Level Five

MUSIC IN ME

A Piano Method for Young Christian Students

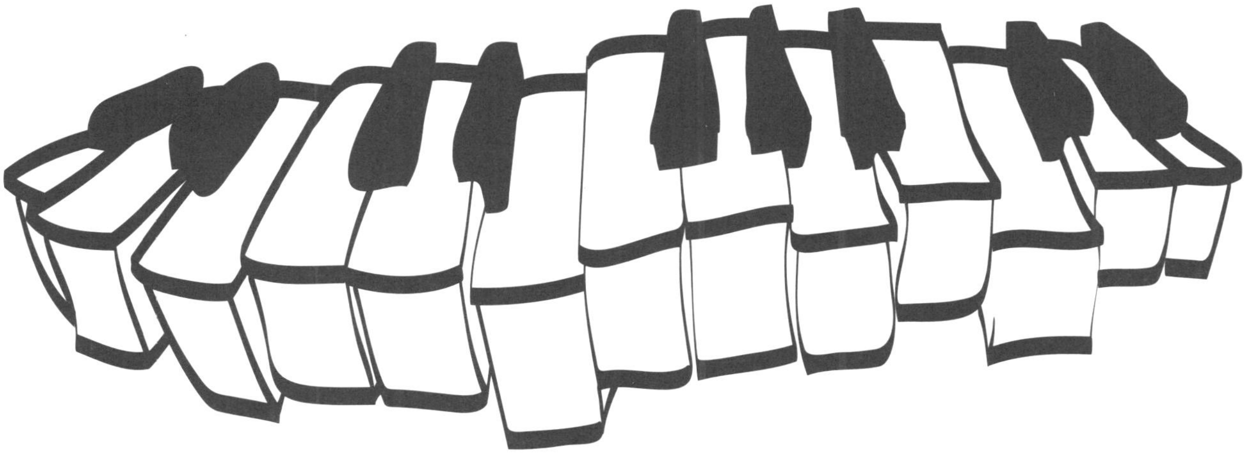

CREATIVITY

(WRITING YOUR OWN MUSIC)

Created by

Carol Tornquist

Illustrations by ED GOBLE
Music Engraving by RIC SIMENSON
Original Cover Design by KIMBERLY SAGMILLER, Visibility Creative

WORD MUSIC

MUSIC IN ME

CONTENTS

"Every good and perfect gift is from above, coming down from the Father of heavenly lights . . . ." (JAMES 1:17)

CREATIVITY

MUSIC IN ME Level One (LESSON) begins with this New Testament scripture about gifts. Music is often called a 'gift' *(something that is 'given')* and good musicians are often called 'gifted' *(having a special talent).*

If you use your TIME to develop your TALENT, your Heavenly Father (through His Holy Spirit) will inspire you to CREATE some amazing music!

So let's get started!

My Toolbox

* abbreviation for ***crescendo*** meaning to play gradually louder

Because the word PSALM means 'sacred song or hymn',
the lyrics of many Christian songs are based upon the Book of Psalms.
(And most were written by the 'chief musician', King David.)

Using some of your musical 'tools', create a melody for the lyrics below based upon Psalm 98:4–5. (See page 14 of your Level Five LESSON Book.)

Shout for Joy to the Lord!

LH ACCOMPANIMENT PATTERNS

You have many choices when it comes to creating LH accompaniments (block chords, broken chords, harmonic intervals, single bass notes, etc.).

- Play the first two bars of the example below. Then, based on the chord symbols, use the ***same broken chord pattern*** to fill in the empty measures that follow.

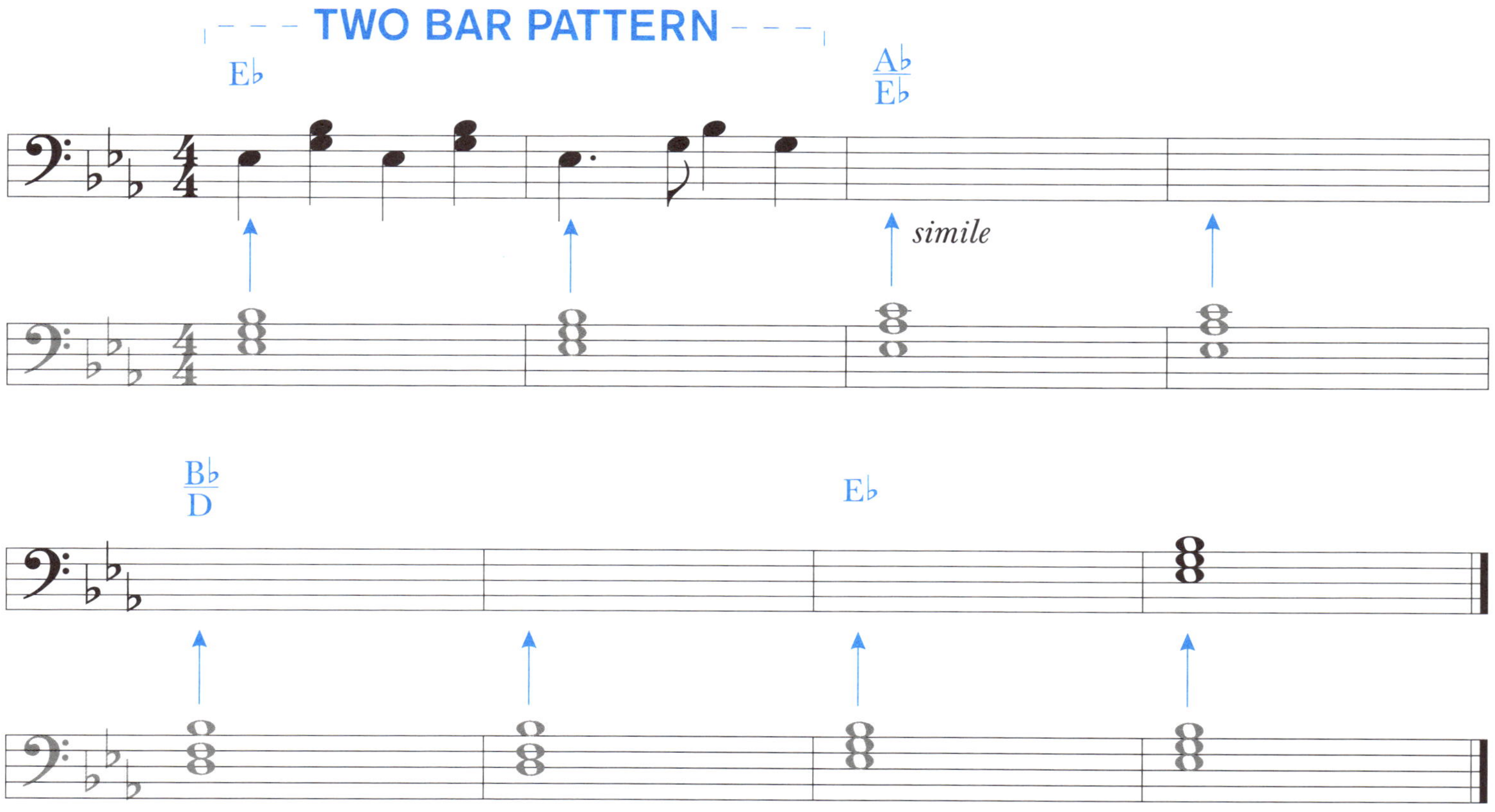

- TRANSPOSE the eight bar broken chord pattern above to the following keys:

F Major

A♭ Major

G Major

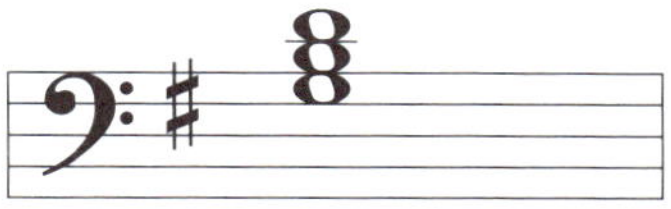

D♭ Major

COMPOUND METER

6/8 is the most familiar time signature in COMPOUND METER.

EIGHTH NOTE (♪) = 1 beat

QUARTER NOTE (♩) = 2 beats

DOTTED QUARTER (♩.) = 3 beats

• Counting six beats per measure, play this happy Italian folk tune!
(Play STUDENT PART **8va** *with duet part.)*

Funiculi, Funicula

Happy!

Italian Air*
LUIGI DENZA, 1880

Optional DUET PART

* 'Air' is another word for *tune.*

Name That Tune!

- Match these two bar phrases with their correct song titles.
  (NOTE: Just 'think' the tune in your mind without playing it.)

1)

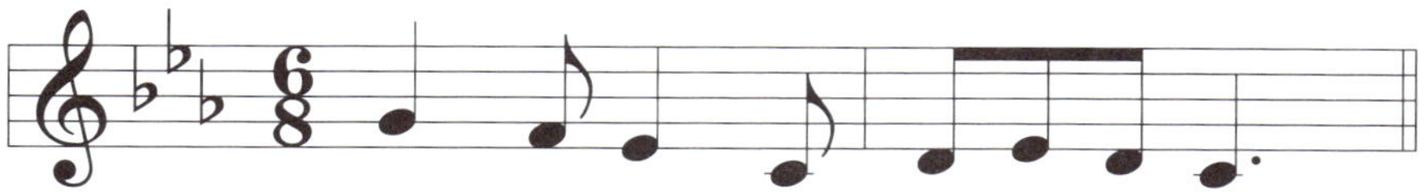

_____ Over the River and Through the Wood

2)

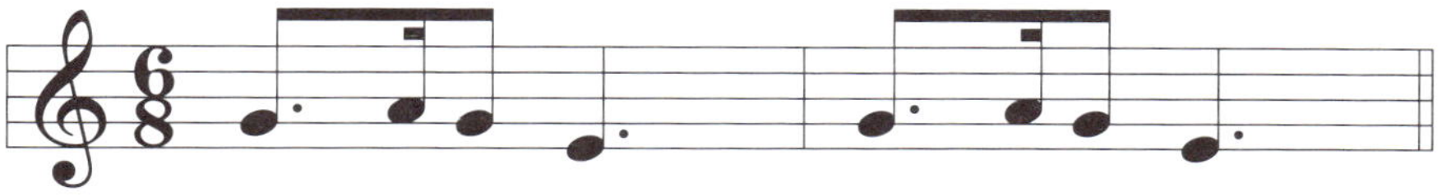

_____ Row, Row, Row Your Boat

3)

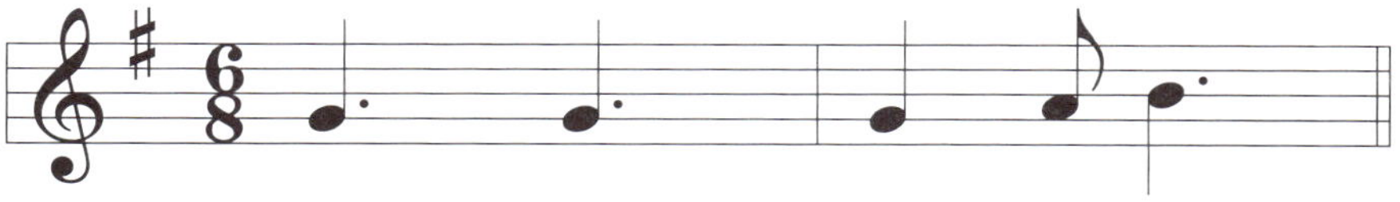

_____ We Three Kings

4)

_____ For He's a Jolly Good Fellow

5)

_____ Silent Night! Holy Night!

6)

_____ Take Me Out to the Ball Game

6/8 RHYTHM PATTERNS

• Using combinations of the following three beat rhythm patterns in COMPOUND METER, complete the four bars of 6/8 meter below. *(No two measures should be the same!)*

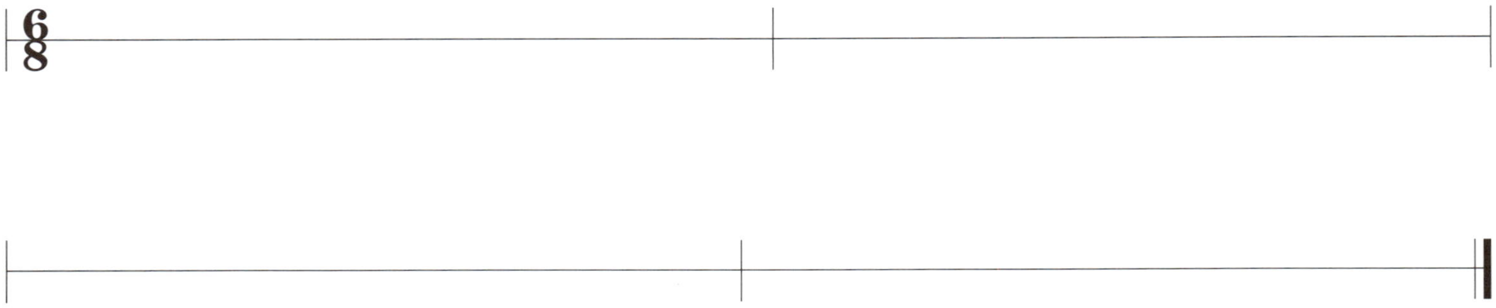

• Then write a four bar melody in the key of E minor using the rhythm patterns that you have created. (Don't forget to end on the tonic: E.)

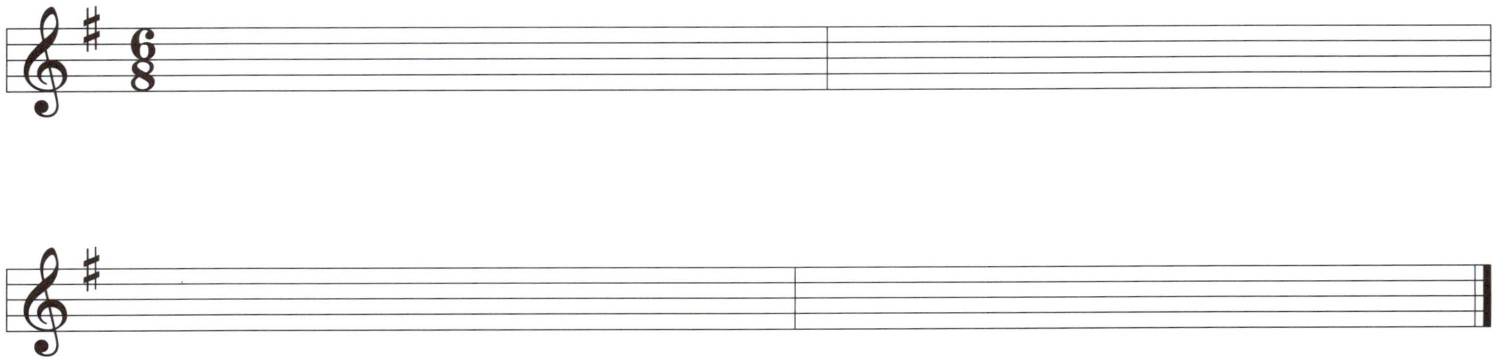

"Shout for joy to the Lord all the earth. Worship the Lord with gladness; come before Him with joyful songs." *(Psalm 100:1–2)*

You have already written a melody on page 4 based on Psalm 98:4 which has the exact same first line of lyrics ***("Shout for joy to the Lord all the earth").*** Here's another 'psalm tune' with similar lyrics, but in COMPOUND METER.

Shout for Joy

(Psalm 100)

GROUP 4 KEYS

The TONIC CHORDS in the GROUP 4 KEYS
Are not all the same… take a look and you'll see!

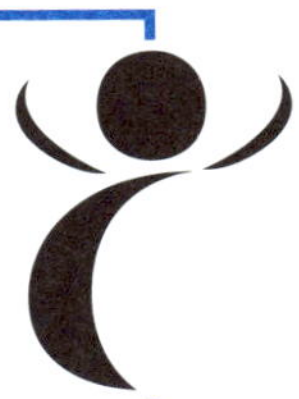

• Write a four bar melody using notes in the TONIC CHORD for each GROUP 4 KEY below.

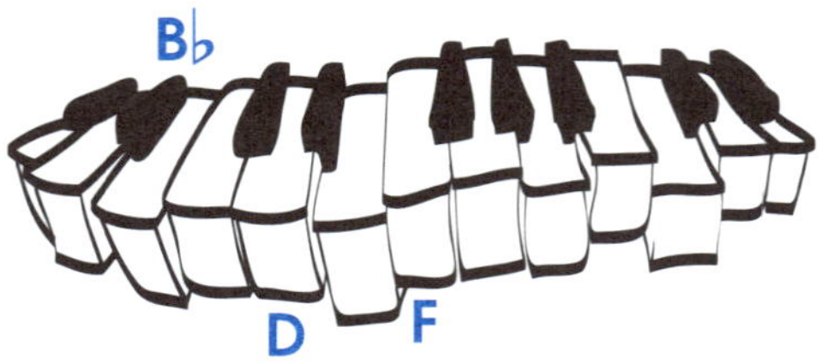

Black White White

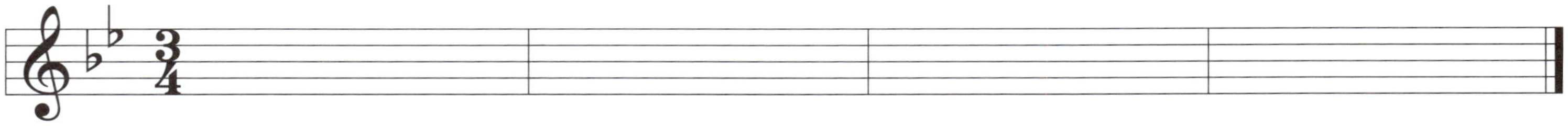

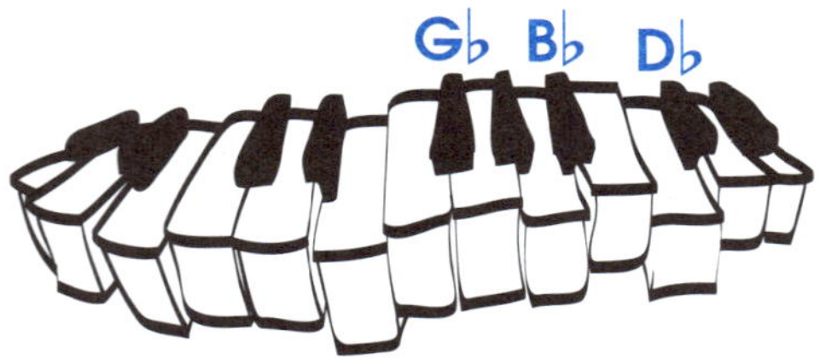

Black Black Black

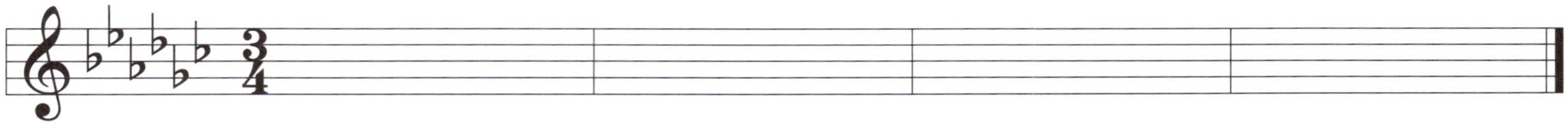

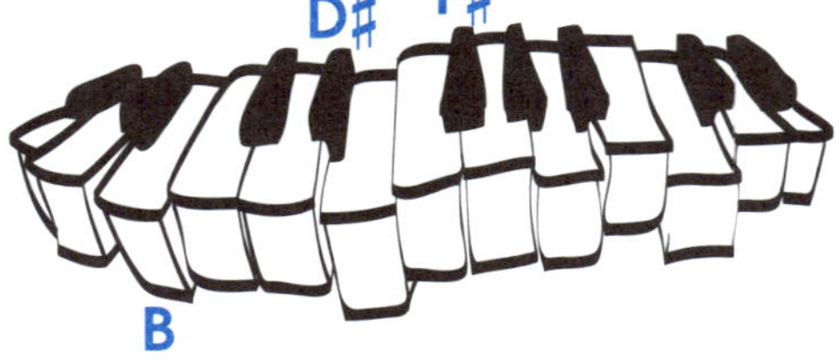

White Black Black

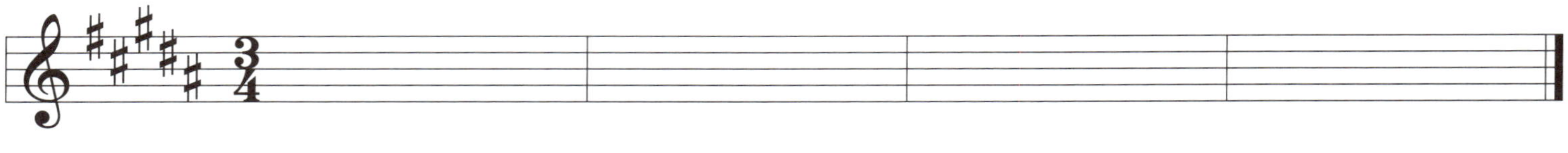

KEY of B♭ MAJOR

• Fill in the MISSING NOTES and LETTER NAMES in both **B♭ MAJOR SCALES** below.

B♭ ___ ___ ___ ___ ___ ___ B♭

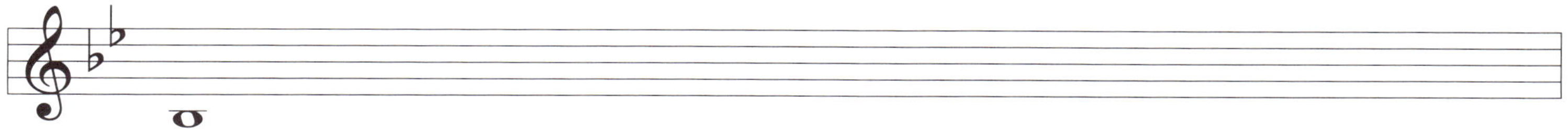

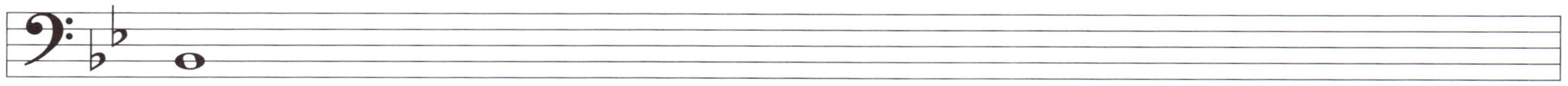

B♭ ___ ___ ___ ___ ___ ___ B♭

Question  Answer

• Create a musical ANSWER for each of the following B♭ Major QUESTIONS.

B♭ MAJOR HAND POSITIONS

In your Level Four CREATIVITY Book (page 10) you played the familiar five finger tune *LIGHTLY ROW* in the key of E♭ Major.

That same tune is notated below in the key of B♭ Major with a broken chord accompaniment.

- Play the arrangement and then describe to your teacher the difference between the melody of the first phrase (bars 1–4) and the second phrase (bars 5–8).

Lightly Row

Traditional

In the traditional melody the first and second lines are very similar (like a simple musical question and answer). But in this arrangement the second line has more 'variety'... especially in bars 6 and 7.

LH CHORDS in B♭ Major

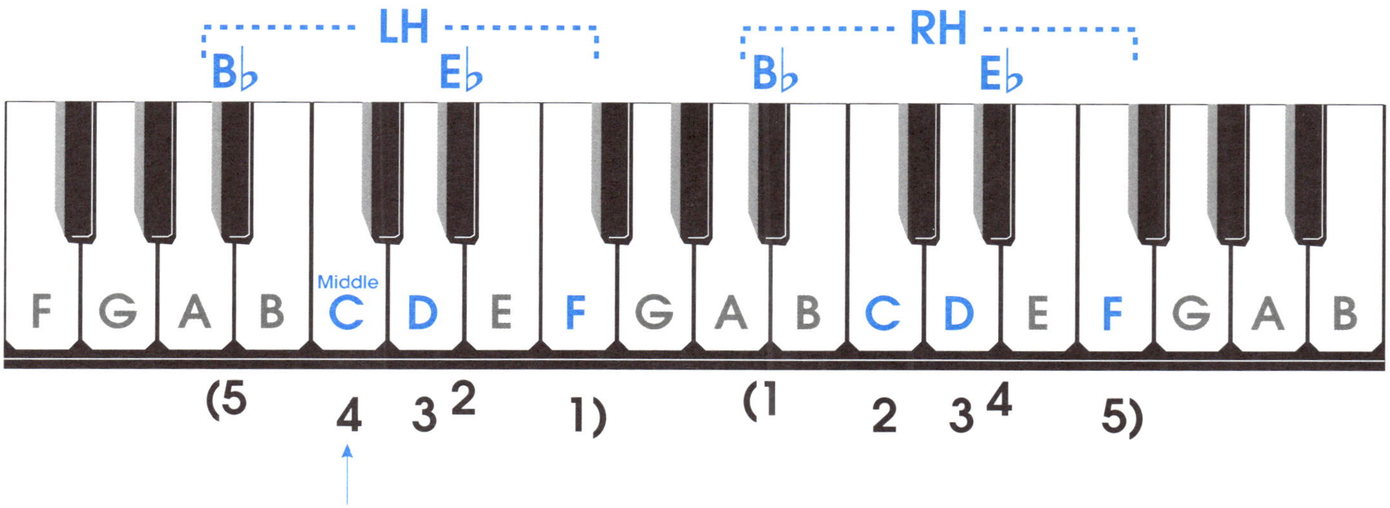

Another 'variation' of *LIGHTLY ROW:*

• In the spaces below describe how the following ELEMENTS OF MUSIC are *different* from page 12.

1) MELODY____

2) CHORDS ____

3) NOTATION_______________________________________

4) RHYTHM____

THEME & VARIATIONS

THEME is another word for a **MELODIC IDEA.**
The simple, basic melody of *LIGHTLY ROW* may be called a THEME.

On page 12 you played a *melodic* VARIATION of that THEME.

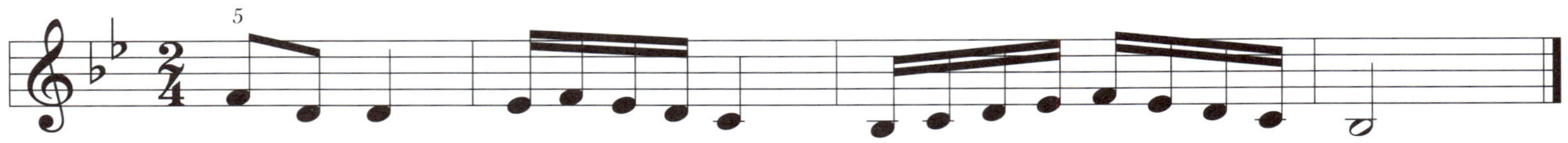

On page 13 you played a *rhythmic* VARIATION.

A third VARIATION includes changes in both the *meter* and the *harmony.*

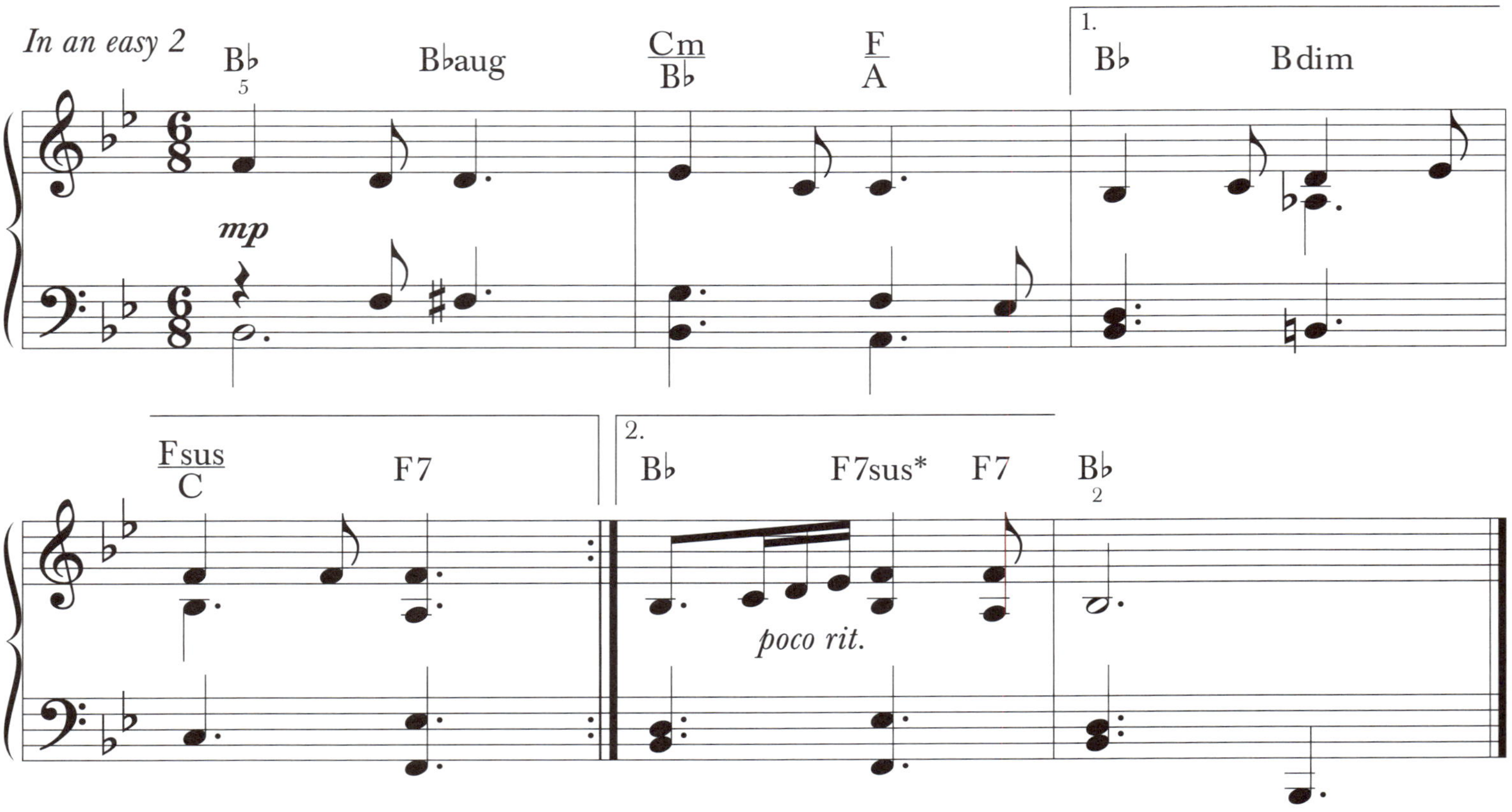

* See Level Five THEORY & TECHNIQUE (page 42).

U–Write!

Just use your IMAGINATION
To write a VARIATION!

• Play the following four bar THEME.

THEME:

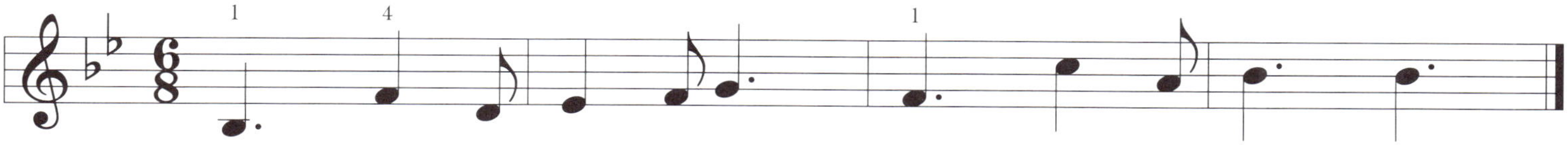

• Now write a VARIATION of the THEME making some slight changes to the melody.

VARIATION 1:

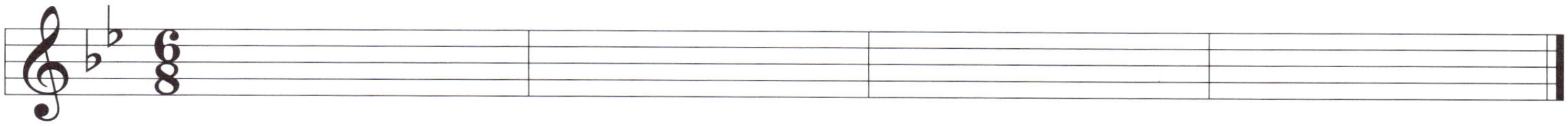

• In the second VARIATION make a few rhythmic changes to the THEME.

VARIATION 2:

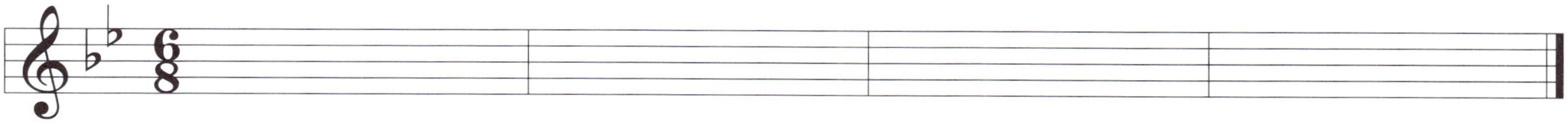

VARIATION 3:

• In the last VARIATION add both a LH accompaniment and chord symbols.
NOTE: You may also want to use some harmonic intervals in the RH.
(See the third VARIATION on page 14.)

RELATIVE MINOR KEYS

- Play each familiar tune below as written in a major key. Then write the same melody below it in its RELATIVE MINOR KEY and listen to the difference!

Joyful, Joyful, We Adore Thee

(G Major)

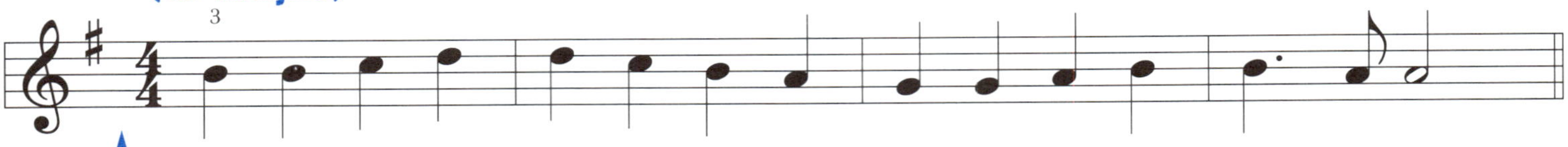

(E minor)

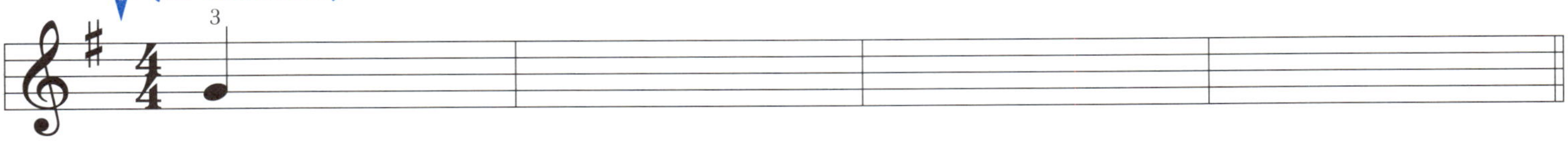

All Hail the Power of Jesus' Name

(E♭ Major)

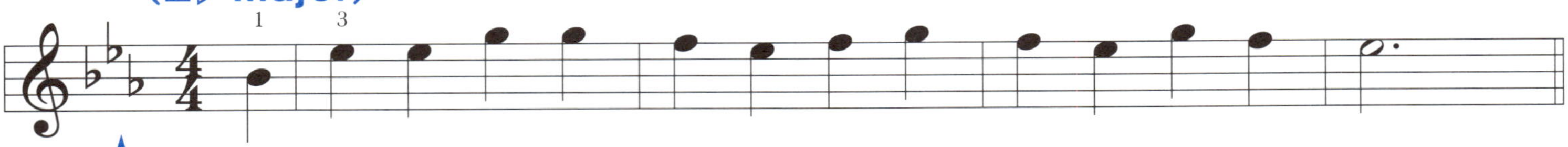

(C minor)

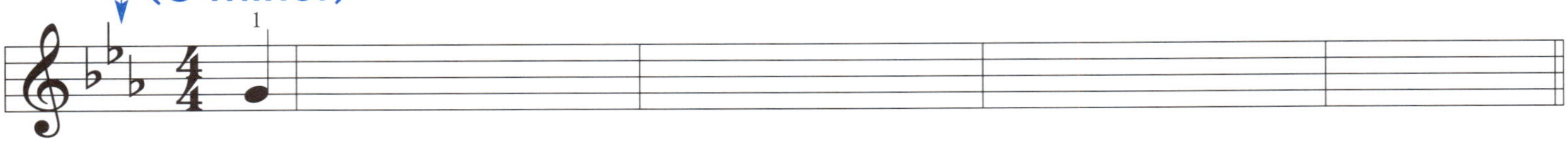

This Little Light of Mine

(D Major)

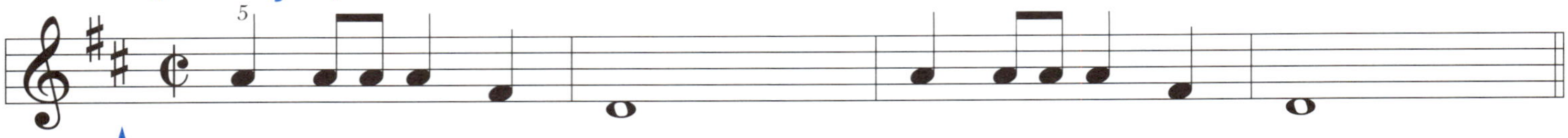

(B minor)

Rejoice in the Lord Always

(B♭ Major)

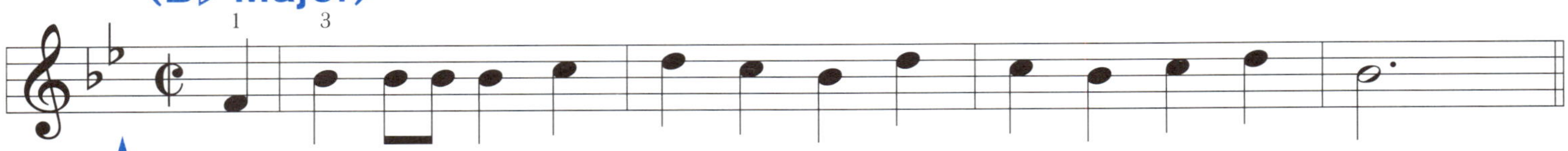

(G minor)

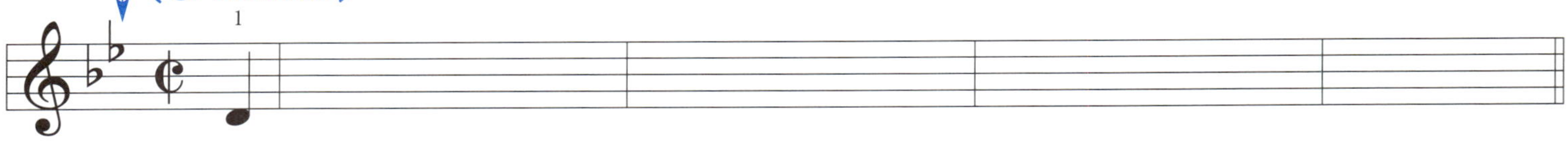

HARMONIC MINOR SCALE

- Play the C **HARMONIC** MINOR SCALE below–
  first with your RH, then with your LH before playing both hands together.

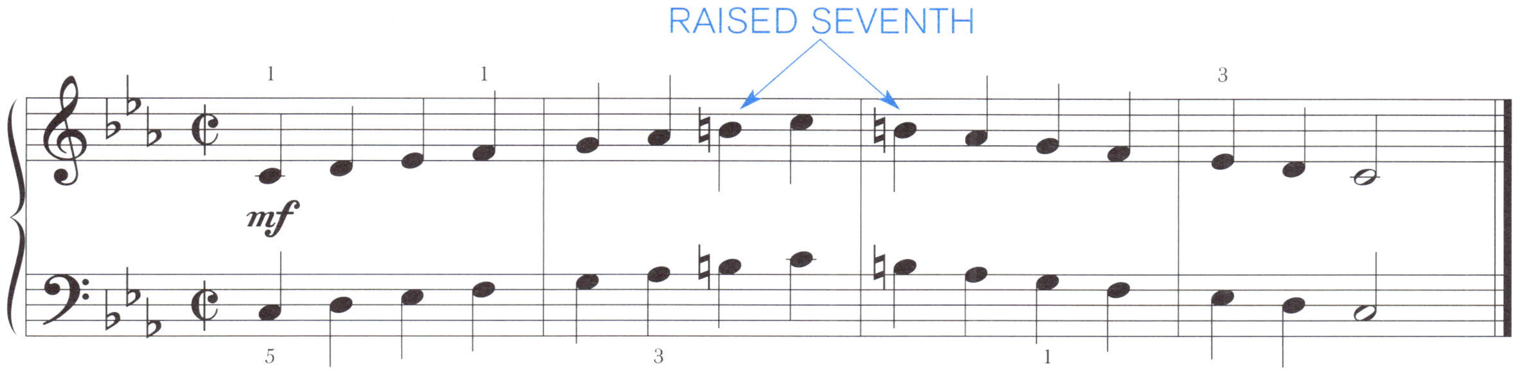

- Add LH harmony to the same RH scale.

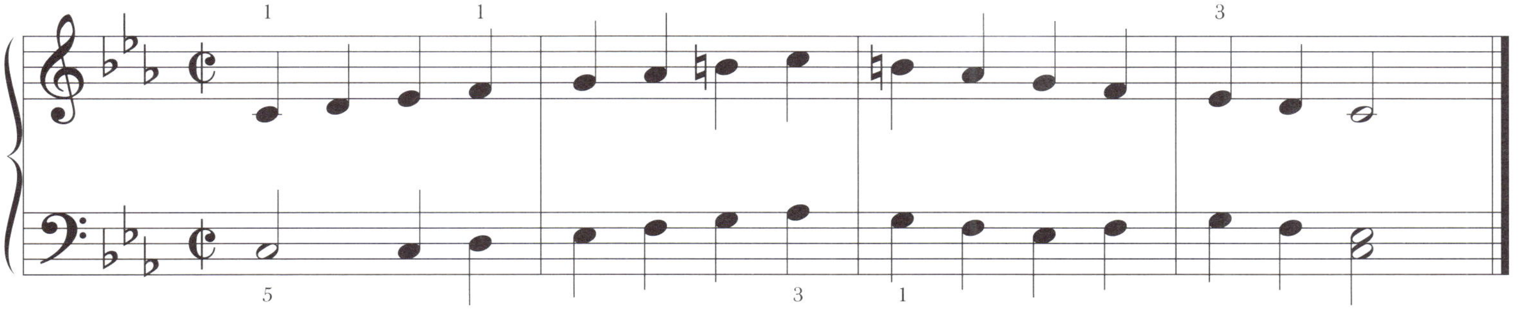

MELODIC MINOR SCALE

- Play the A **MELODIC** MINOR SCALE below–
  first with your RH, then with your LH before playing both hands together.

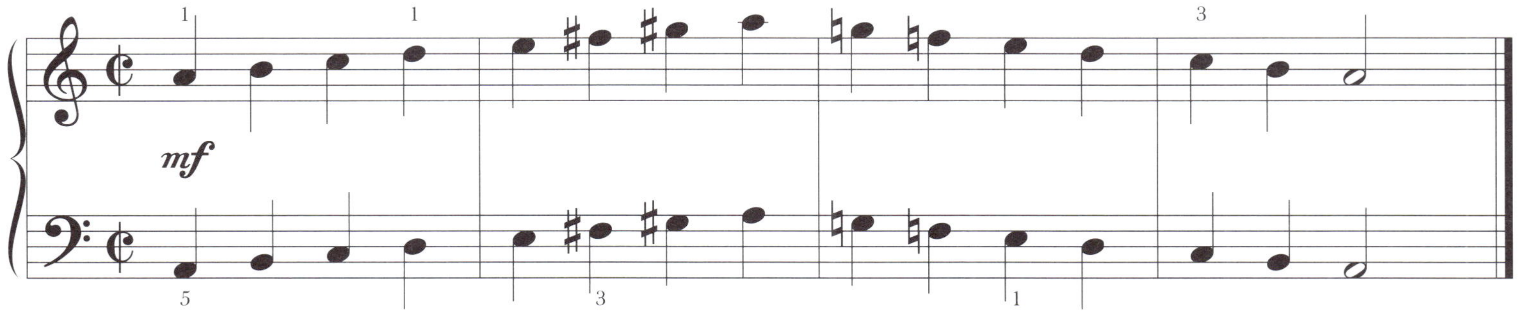

- Add the missing accidentals to the A MELODIC MINOR SCALE below.
  Then play what you have written.

EAR TRAINING
(Melodic Dictation)

- Listen carefully as your teacher plays short melodies in SIX DIFFERENT MINOR KEYS (always beginning on the TONIC). Since each tune is in a different meter, pay close attention to the TIME SIGNATURE as well. Then write what you hear.

(D minor)

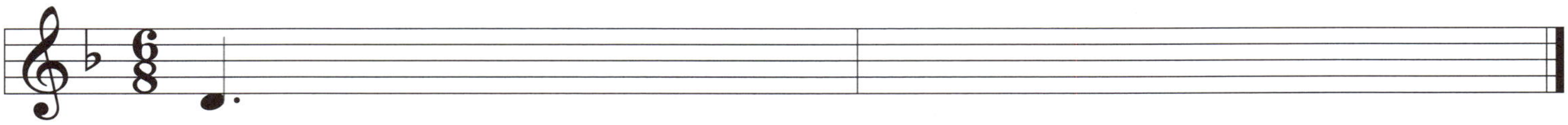

(F minor)

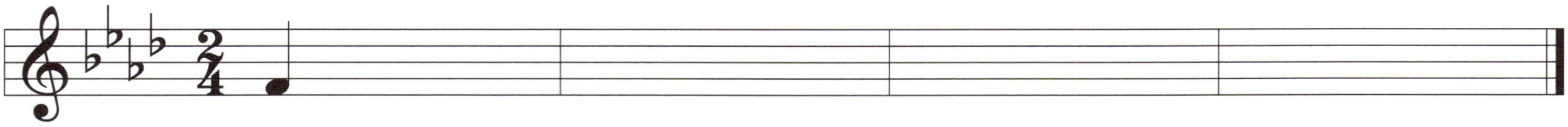

(E minor)

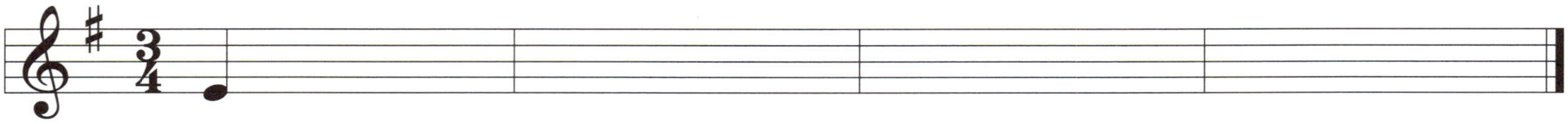

(B minor)

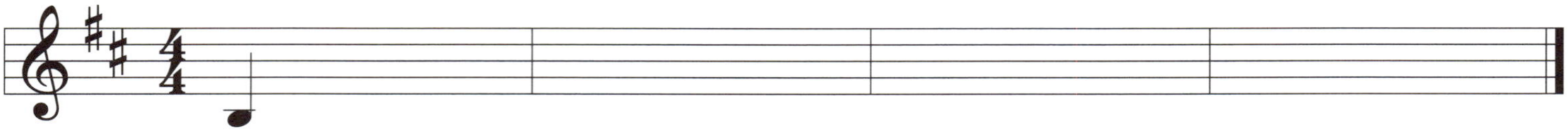

(C minor)

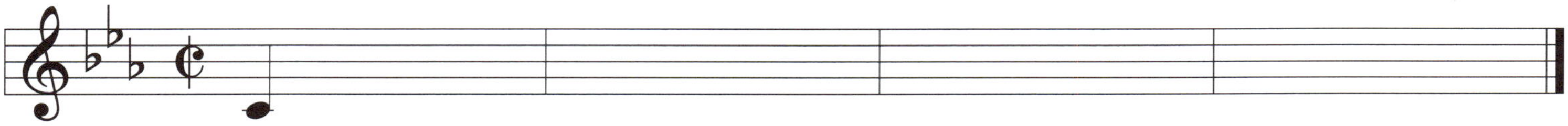

(F♯ minor)

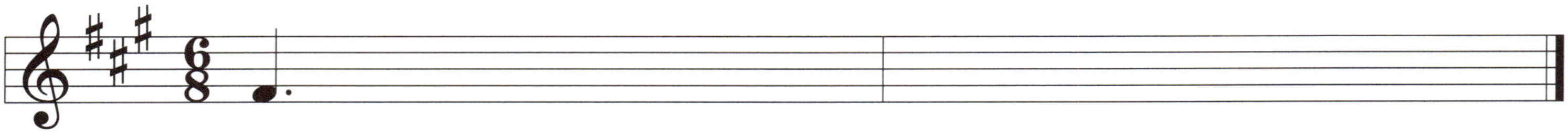

In his gospel, Matthew recalled the words of the Old Testament prophet, Isaiah, concerning the birth of Jesus:

"The virgin will be with child and will give birth to a Son, and they will call Him Immanuel which means 'God with us'." (MATTHEW 1:23)

During the season of Advent (four weeks before Christmas) we prepare for the coming of Immanuel.

- Create a melody and LH accompaniment for bars 3–8 to complete the Advent song below.

God with Us, Immanuel

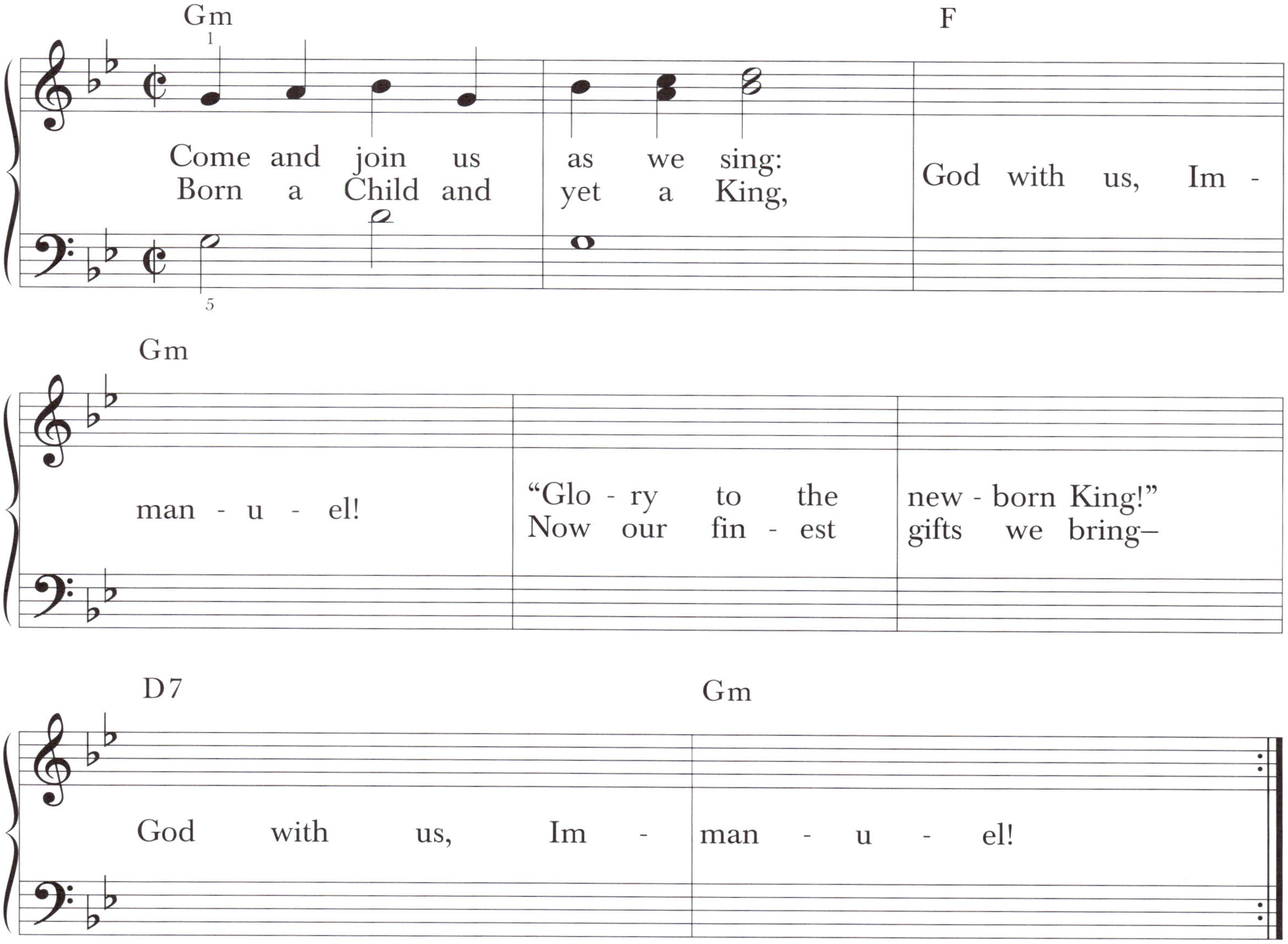

Seeing music *in a circle* always helps to understand
That all things are in order in the great Creator's plan.
Just move in FIFTHS around the circle—start and end on C;
And soon you'll 'get the picture' of how music came to be!

- Fill in the LETTER NAMES of the major keys below… always counting ahead a PERFECT FIFTH.

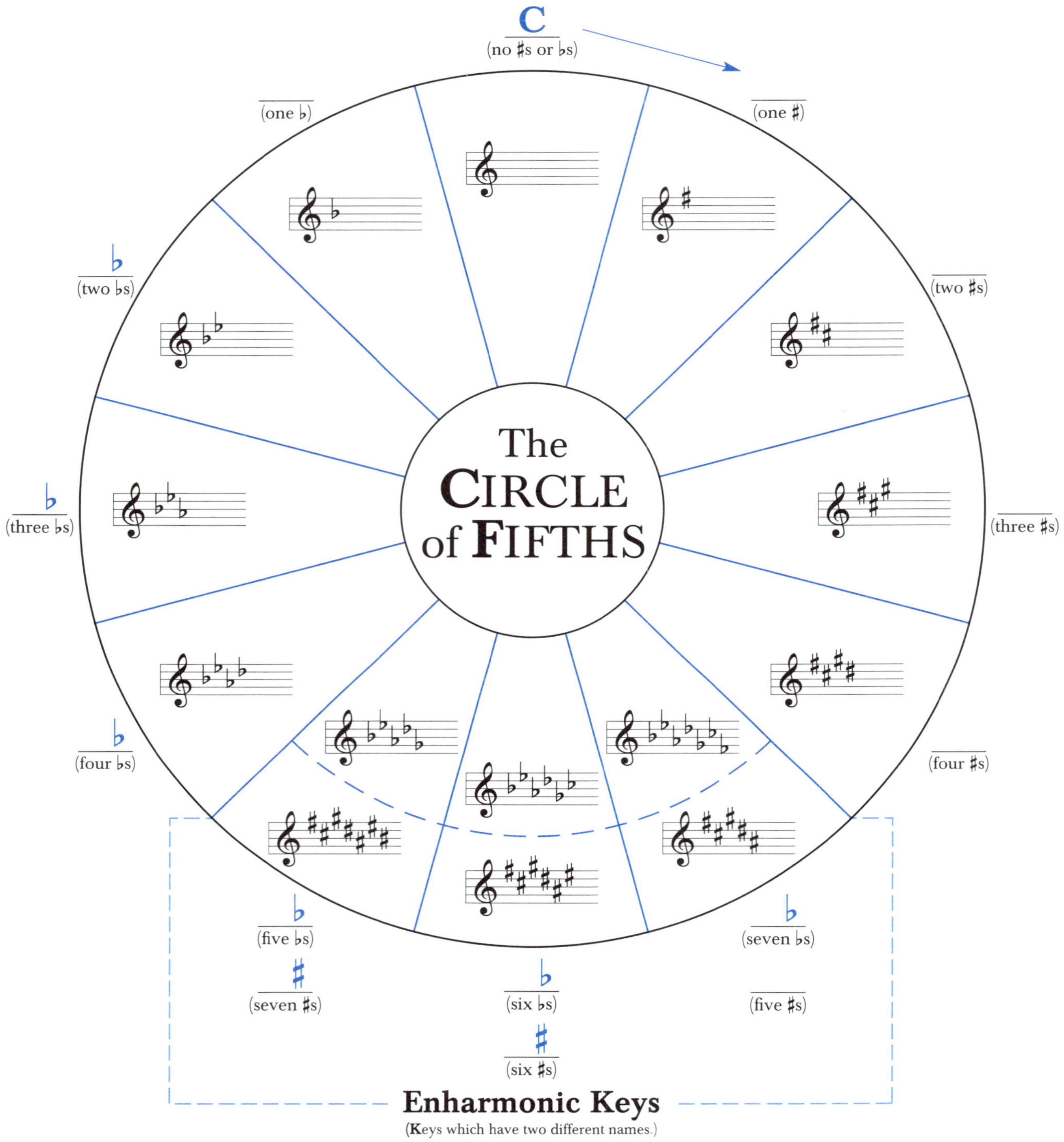

(You may check your answers by looking at the CIRCLE of FIFTHS on page 20 of your Level Five LESSON Book.)

"But everything should be done in a fitting and orderly way."

(I Corinthians 14:40)

The ORDER of FLATS

By looking at the CIRCLE of FIFTHS on page 20 and moving *counter–clockwise* (from C to C) you can easily see the **ORDER of FLATS.** (You will move in **PERFECT FOURTHS** instead of FIFTHS.)

- Write a four bar melody in the key of F Major beginning and ending on the TONIC.

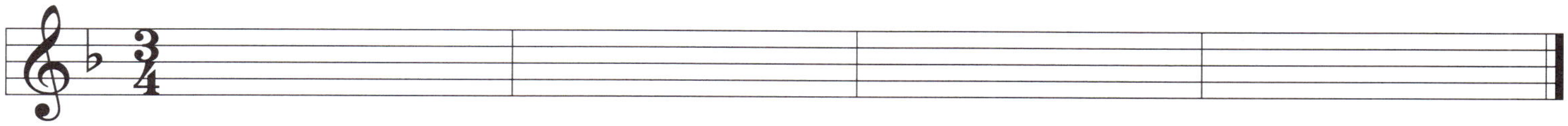

- Then write the same tune adding the KEY SIGNATURE in each of the following flat keys:

B♭ Major

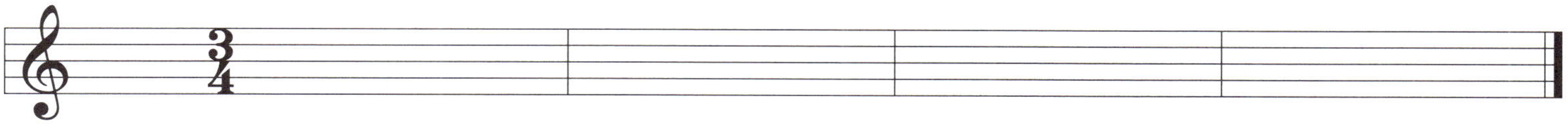

E♭ Major

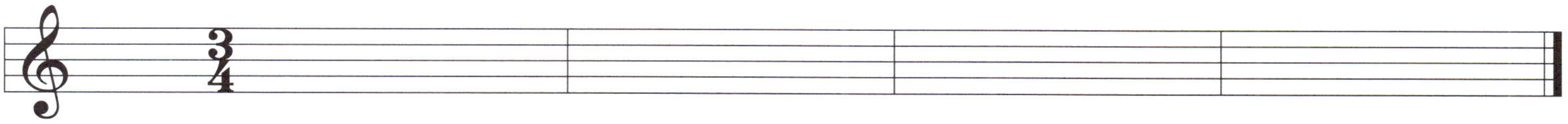

A♭ Major

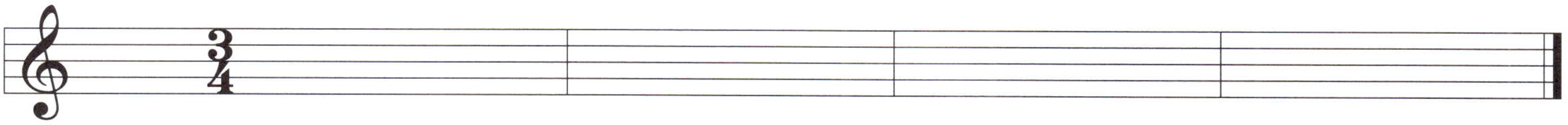

D♭ Major

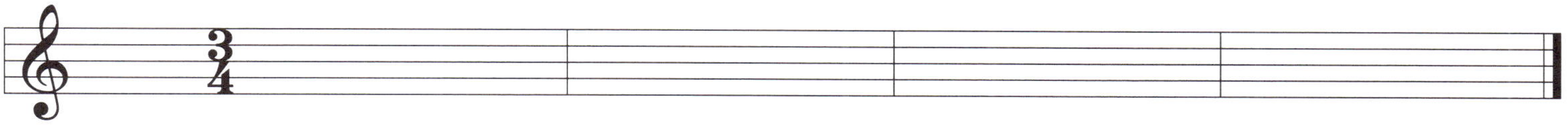

KEY of G♭ MAJOR

C♭ (white key)

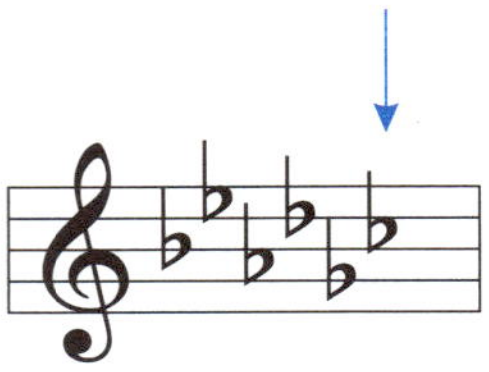

Six flats... *imagine that!*
One is white and the rest are black!

Playing a really 'fun' tune is a great way to get your fingers accustomed to playing on the black keys. *(Your RH doesn't play a single white key in the whole song!)*

Serendipity*

* SERENDIPITY refers to making an interesting discovery. You may 'discover' that you can play this song by rolling your right fist across the black notes!

G♭ MAJOR HAND POSITIONS

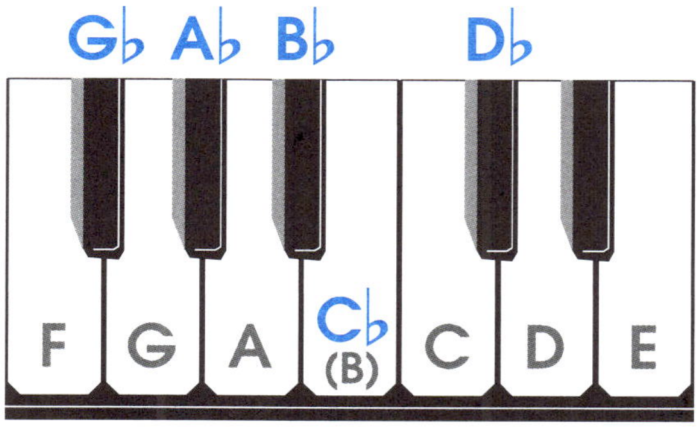

• With your RH in the G♭ MAJOR HAND POSITION, play the five finger tune below.

Song title*

____

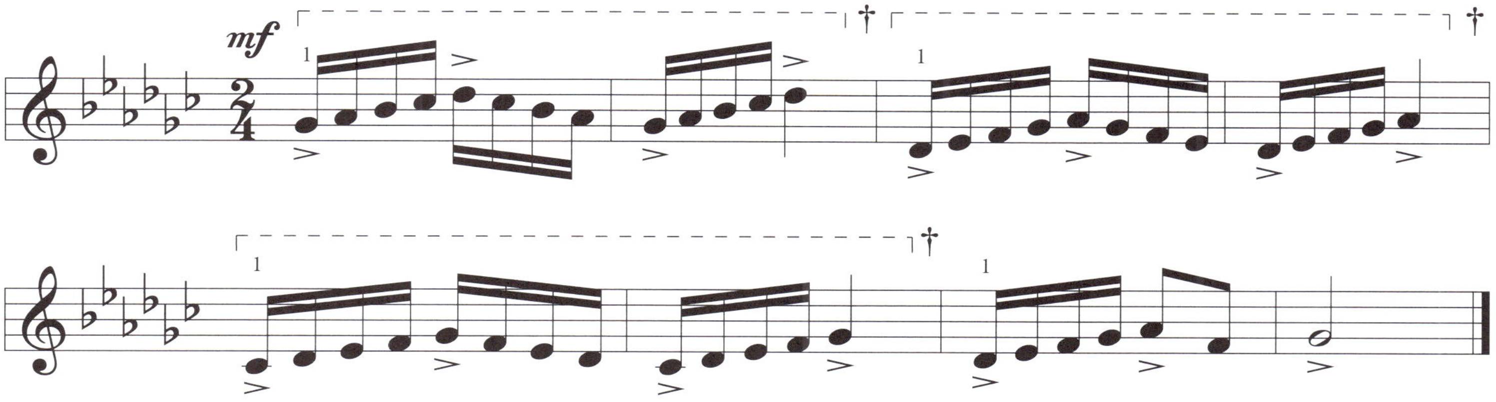

• With your LH in the G♭ MAJOR HAND POSITION (8vb), play the same eight bars 'by ear'.

* Can you think of a fun song title to describe this tune? (Think about the rhythm, tempo and direction of the melody.)

If you're stumped for an idea,
If your mind can't 'get a grip',
Here's a list of some suggestions
Just in case you need a hint!

1) *FIVE FINGER FRENZY*
2) *SLOW 'MO'*
3) *GONE FISHIN'*
4) *MUSIC IN MOTION*

Add one of these titles, (or even better, a title YOU create) to the line above the song.

† **SEQUENCE**– same tune beginning on a different note (See page 33 of your Level Five THEORY & TECHNIQUE Book.)

LH CHORDS in G♭ Major

- Using just two of the PRIMARY CHORDS in the new key of G♭ MAJOR, create a LH accompaniment for this traditional chorus.

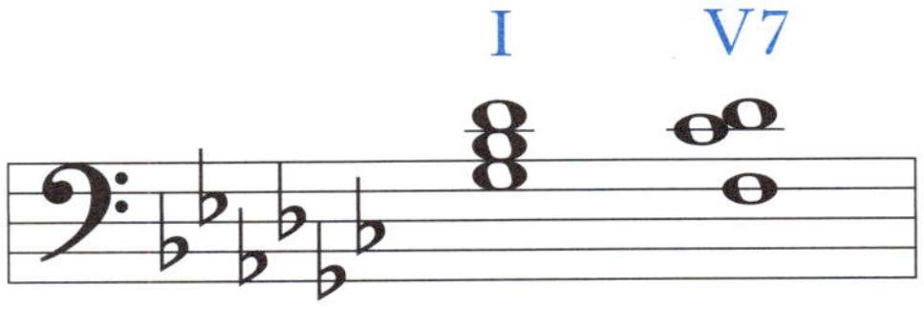

"Be joyful always; pray continually; give thanks in all circumstances, for this is God's will for you in Christ Jesus." *(I THESSALONIANS 5:16)*

Down in My Heart*
(I've Got the Joy)

Traditional

* Sometimes this tune is called *I'VE GOT THE JOY IN MY HEART* or simply *I'VE GOT THE JOY.*

You can play a lot of songs with just two chords **(I and V7).**
Here's the beginning of *HE'S GOT THE WHOLE WORLD IN HIS HANDS.*
Can you play the rest 'by ear'?
(If you aren't familiar with this tune ask your teacher to suggest another one.)

You can play even more songs by adding the **IV CHORD.**

- Choose your own harmonies (I, IV, V or V7).
  Then add chord symbols above the treble staff for the last three lines.

Amazing Grace

Traditional American melody

This is probably the most popular hymn of all!
Can you name some places where you have heard it played and sung?

AB (Binary) FORM

You have just played *AMAZING GRACE* which is not only an extremely popular hymn, but a very short one as well. However, it does have five verses. (And sometimes singers add a sixth verse with the lyrics: *"Praise God"* repeated over and over again.)

But many longer hymns have two parts (VERSE and CHORUS). This is known as **AB (Binary) FORM.**

The hymn below in AB FORM is probably the very first hymn that you ever learned!

- Play the RH melody first. Then create a simple LH accompaniment.

"Christ loved us and gave Himself for us...." (EPHESIANS 5:2)

The word **INTERLUDE** usually refers to a short musical piece played between one part of a worship service and the next. An INTERLUDE often does not even have a melody, but may just be a simple chord progression like the one below.

Notice that the RH part is made up of **BROKEN CHORDS** throughout, while the LH is a single note pattern with a **G♭ BASS NOTE** in every measure.

Interlude in G♭ Major

* *cresc. poco a poco*—**crescendo** (play louder) little by little
decresc. poco a poco—**decrescendo** (play softer) little by little

ABA (Ternary) FORM

Songs in **ABA (Ternary) FORM** usually begin with the CHORUS. Then comes a VERSE before the song repeats back to (and ends on) the CHORUS. An ending (or CODA) is often added as well.

NOTE: The TEACHER'S PART of this duet arrangement is written below, but the STUDENT'S PART is on page 29.

Go, Tell It on the Mountain
(Duet)

Traditional Spiritual

CHORUS

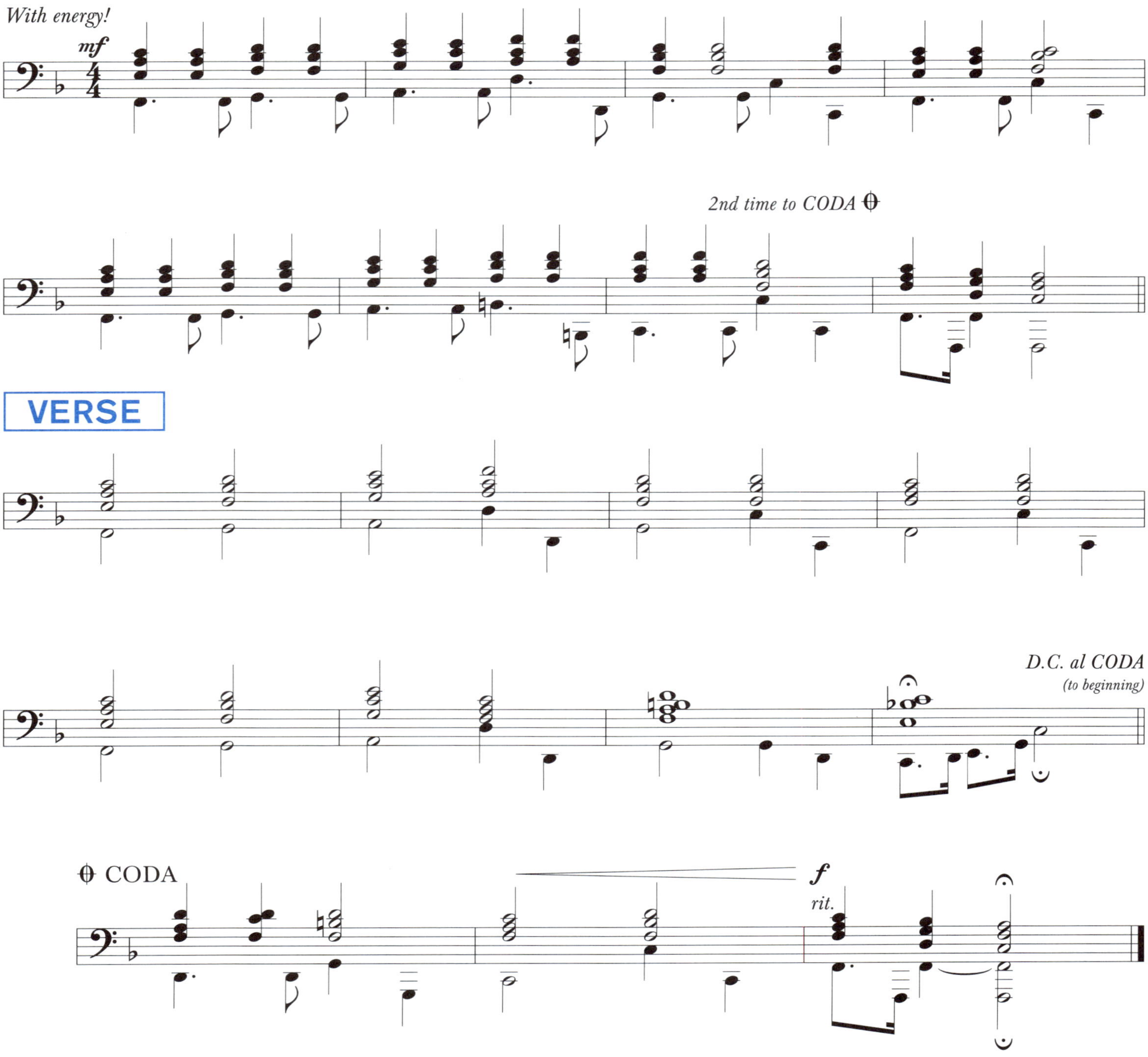

"...let them shout from the mountaintops.
Let them give glory to the Lord...." (ISAIAH 42:11–12)

STUDENT PART (8va)

Go, Tell It on the Mountain
(Duet)

CHORUS

With energy!

Traditional Spiritual

VERSE

NOTE: There is also a solo arrangement of this spiritual in your Level Five HYMNS & HOLIDAYS Book (pages 26–27).

CHROMATICALLY Speaking...

• Fill in the BASS CLEF NOTES below which should be an exact 'echo' of the RH tune. (Include the ACCIDENTALS and FINGERINGS, too.)

Echo-ology

ECHO-OLOGY is also made of **SEQUENCES** (same tunes starting on different notes).

Which RH measure(s) is (or are) *a sequence of the first measure?* _____

How many measures in the whole song have *exactly the same rhythm pattern?* _____

U-Write!

The melody below is a *combination* of both MAJOR and CHROMATIC scale patterns—*plus* SEQUENCES.

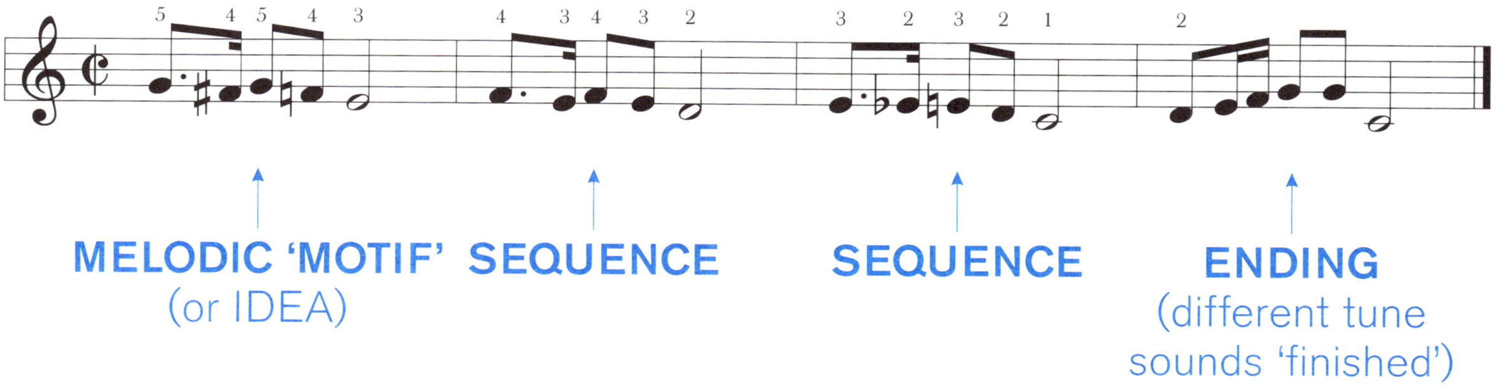

• Using the same four bar pattern as above, create your own melody.

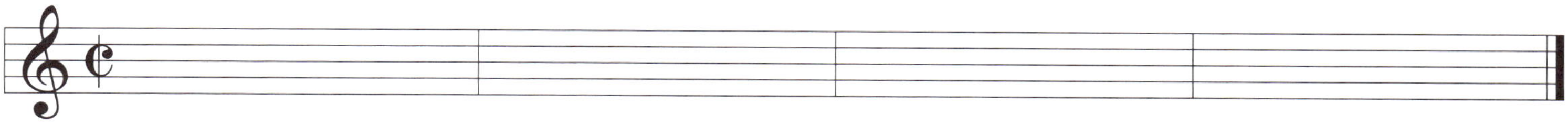

Here is another 'MOTIF' (idea) that expands into an eight bar bass line.

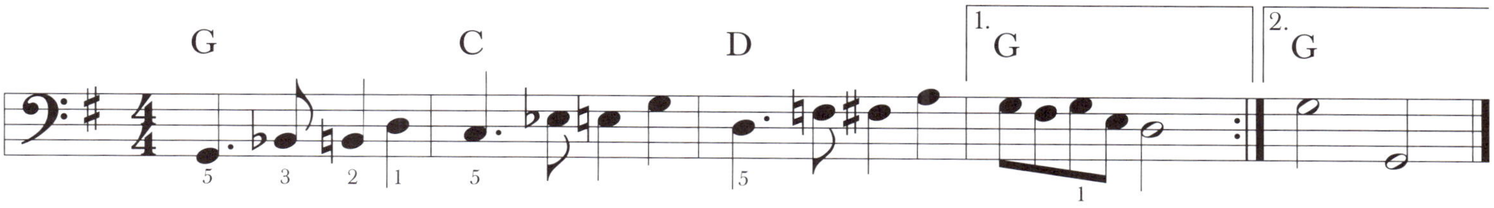

The **CHORD SYMBOLS** are included in case you want to *improvise* a RH part using the **I, IV and V CHORDS** in the key of G Major.

For example:

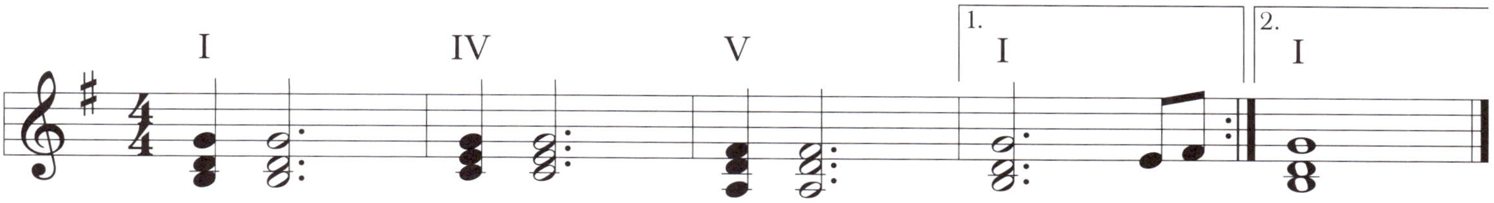

KEY of B MAJOR

You already know the pattern of HALF and WHOLE STEPS in any major scale.

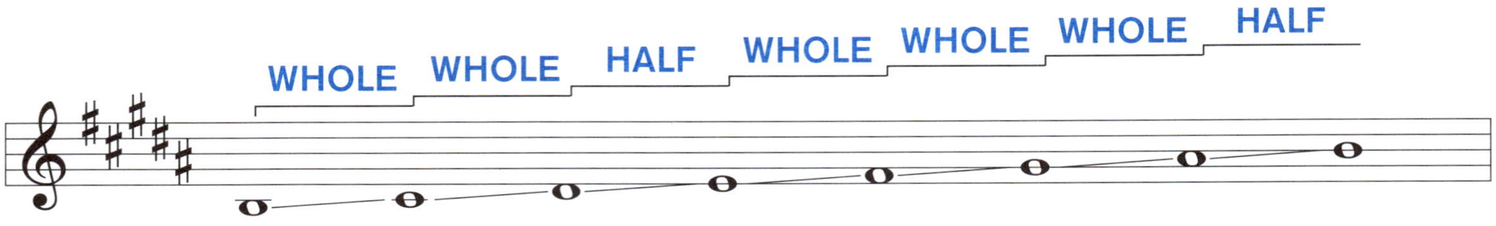

Every major scale also includes two TETRACHORDS
(identical groups of four successive notes).

• Play the following **'TETRACHORD TUNES'.**

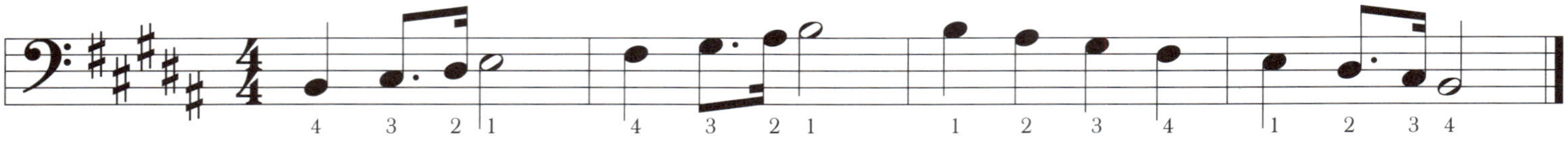

• Create your own 'TETRACHORD TUNE' in $\frac{3}{4}$ time.

In JOHN *13:34 Jesus said:* **"A new command I give you: Love one another. As I have loved you, so you must love one another."**

Using a *simple five finger melody* is a good way to communicate this *simple Biblical truth:*

Love one another.

(Remember that *"loving our neighbors as ourselves"* is also one of the two greatest commandments!)

- With both hands in the **B MAJOR HAND POSITION,** play this traditional melody with new lyrics *straight from the Gospel of John.*

Love One Another*

* This same tune was also used for *SING ALLELUIA* (Level Two CREATIVITY, page 27) and *THIS IS THE DAY* (Level Two LESSON, page 29).

In your Level Five THEORY & TECHNIQUE Book (page 34) you are playing a new BROKEN CHORD PATTERN. (It's called playing 'in tenths' because the highest note of the arpeggio is *ten notes higher* than the lowest bass note.)

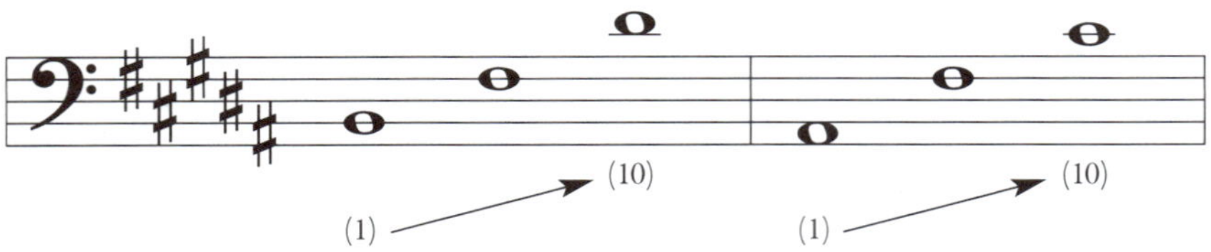

Practice the LH broken chord pattern on the bass staff below until you can play it comfortably. (Remember to change your pedal each time the chord changes.)

- Then write the melody of *LOVE ONE ANOTHER* on the treble staff below *one octave higher* than you just played it on page 33, and play both hands together.

Love One Another

This arrangement is written in $\frac{9}{8}$ so that you can easily hear the difference between SIMPLE and COMPOUND METER.

Think 'in 3' as you play.

My Country, 'Tis of Thee

Thesaurus Musicus

Because 12/8 meter is counted 'in 4',

()

many songs in 4/4 time may be adapted to this compound time signature.

You can easily *hear the difference* between 4/4 and 12/8 time in this example from *TWINKLE, TWINKLE, LITTLE STAR.*

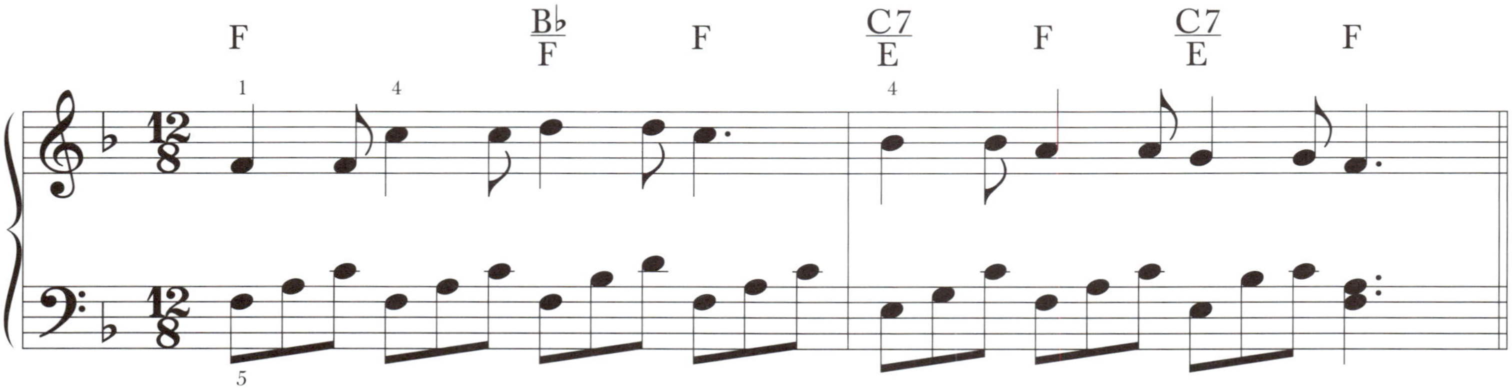

• Reading the chord symbols, write an EIGHTH NOTE ACCOMPANIMENT for *JOYFUL, JOYFUL, WE ADORE THEE* similar to the one above.

• Complete the first two bars of the RH MELODY in *JESUS LOVES ME.* Then play what you have written.

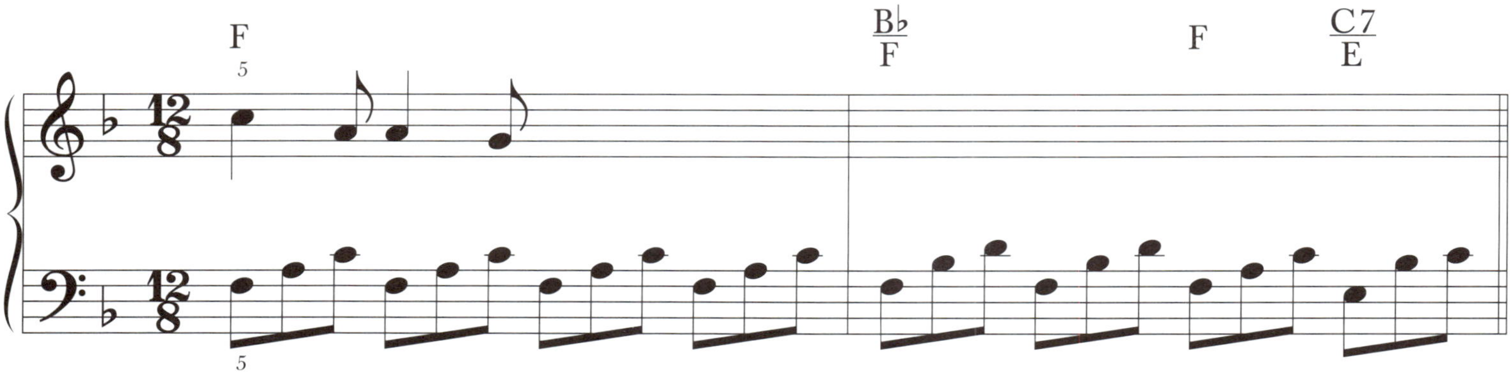

SECONDARY CHORDS

• Play *COME INTO HIS PRESENCE* with the primary chord symbols below.

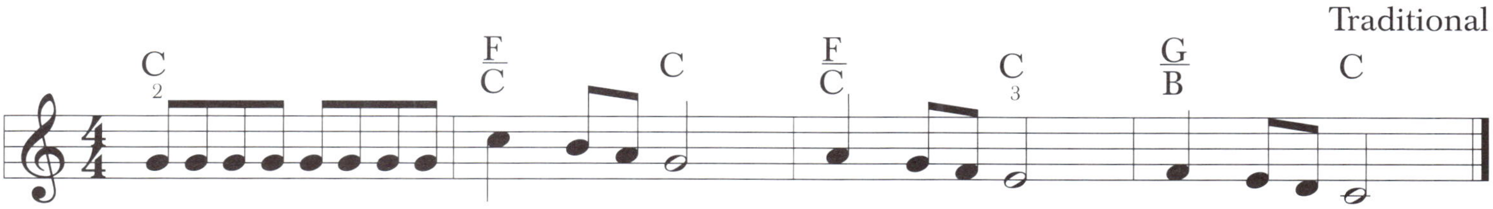

Now that you know how to play in all of the major keys, you are ready to work with more of your musical 'tools'— *especially* **SECONDARY CHORDS (II, III, VI and VII).**

• Try the same song again with a more 'interesting' accompaniment!

Come into His Presence

• Add the correct ROMAN NUMERAL for each chord in the chord progression above.

C (I) Em ( ) Am ( ) F ( ) C ( )

Dm ( ) G ( ) C ( ) Dm ( ) G7 ( ) C ( )

EAR TRAINING

- Close your eyes and listen carefully as your teacher plays the following **TWO MEASURE CHORD PROGRESSIONS** using both PRIMARY and SECONDARY CHORDS. Then circle which one you heard (A or B).

A

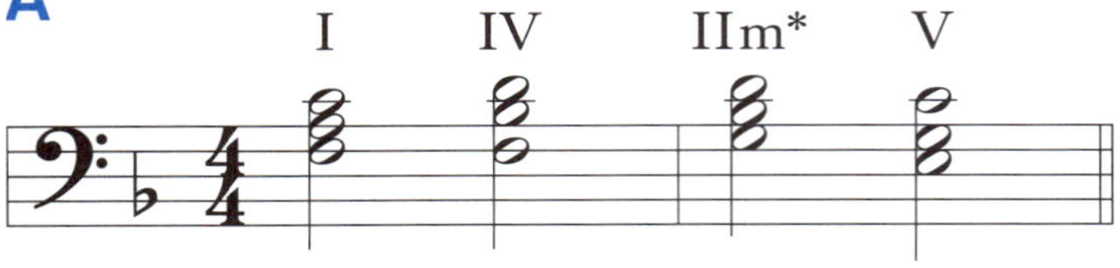

B

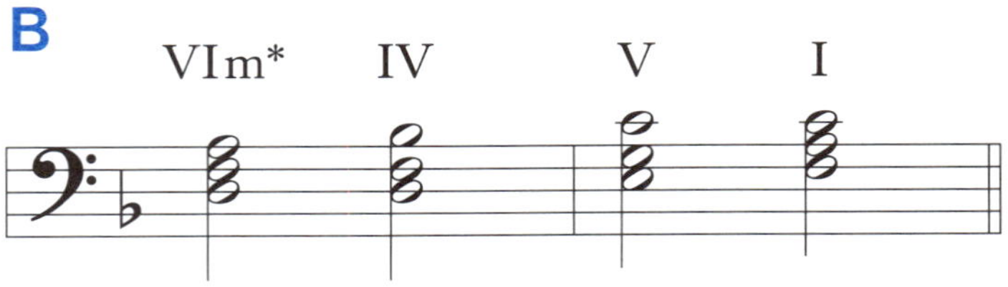

A

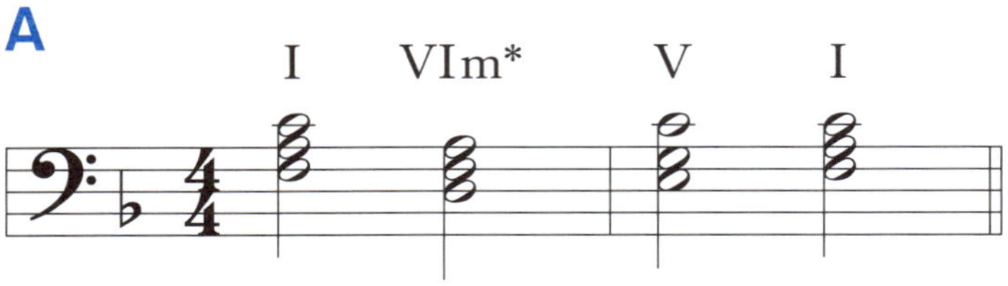

B

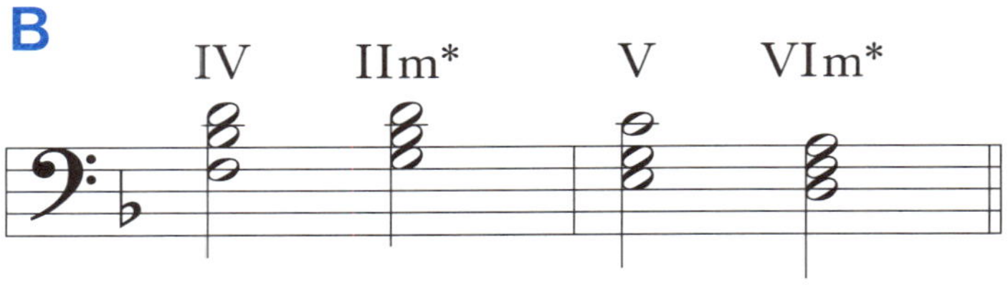

A

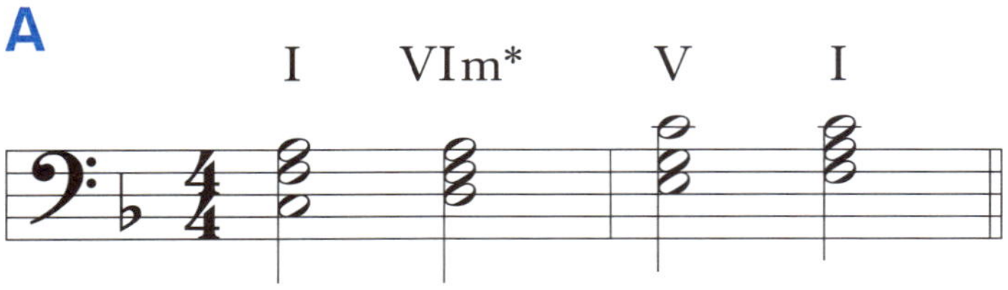

B

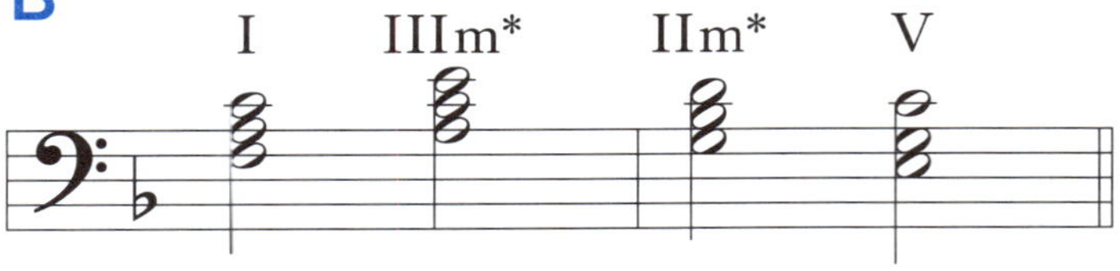

* All minor chords (II, III and VI) are indicated by a lower case 'm' (IIm, IIIm and VIm).

Harmonic Dictation

Your teacher will play a progression of just TWO CHORDS (broken and block).

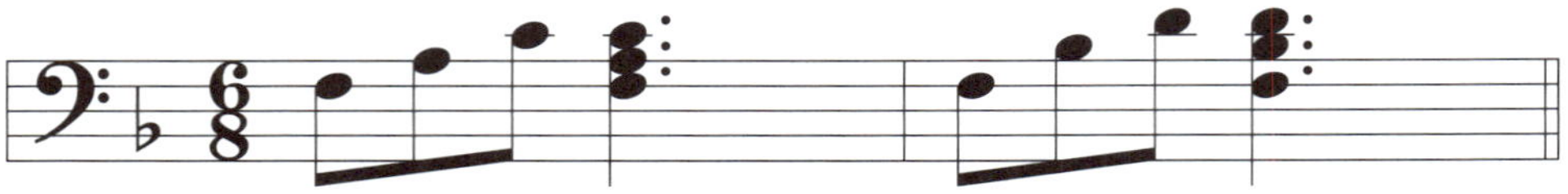

- Listen carefully and then write each progression below (both beginning on F).

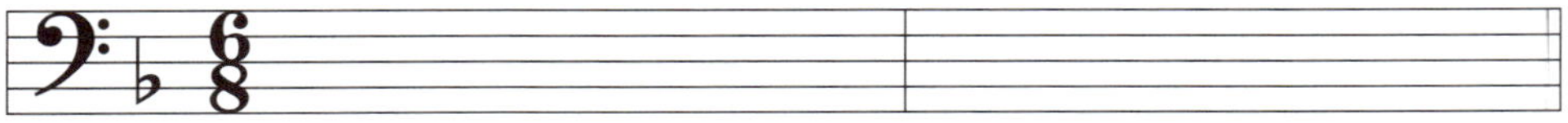

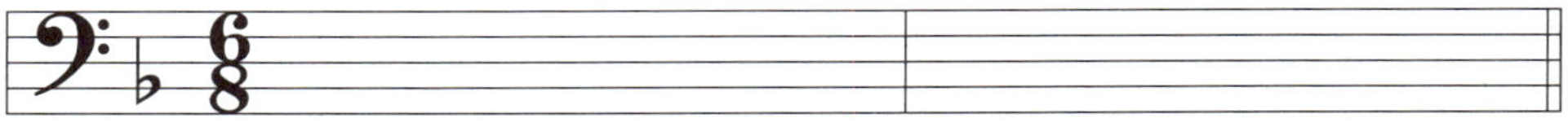

INTERVALS in the MAJOR SCALE

• Create a musical 'answer' to each 'question' below using **PERFECT** and **MAJOR INTERVALS** in the G major scale.

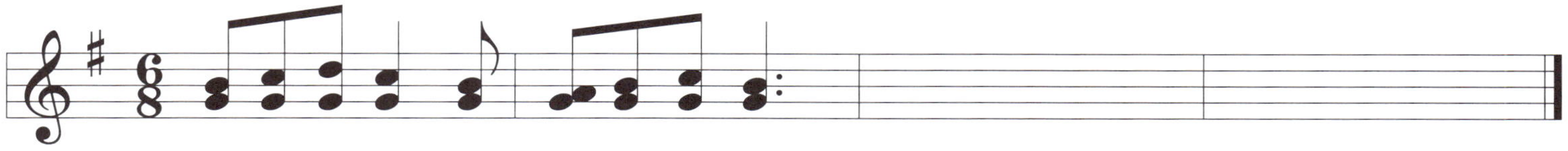

INTERVALS in the MINOR SCALE

In any minor scale there are three types of interval:
MINOR, MAJOR and **PERFECT.**

• Create a musical 'question' for each 'answer' in the key of **E minor (RELATIVE MINOR of G major).**

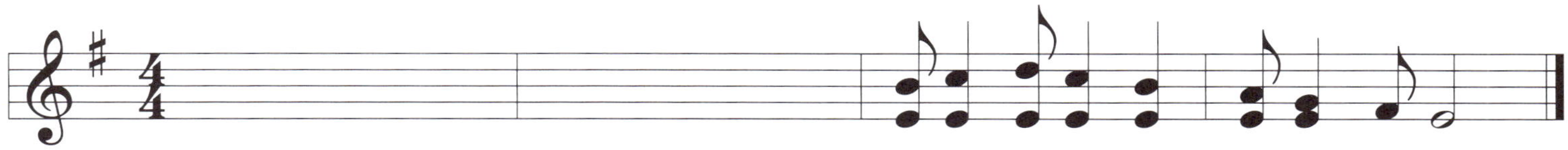

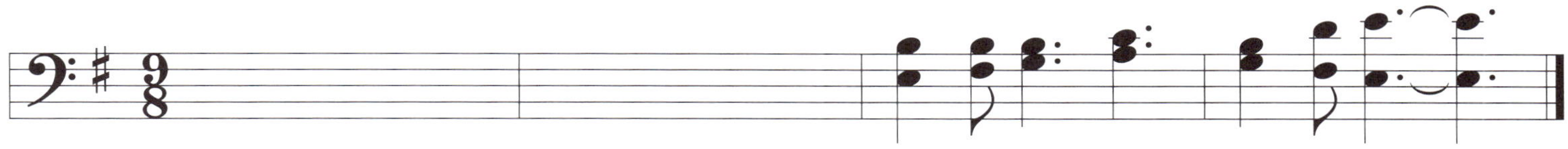

"Worship the Lord in the splendor of His holiness." *(I Chronicles 16:29)*

- Play bars 1–8 of this traditional worship chorus. Notice that the RH part is made up of INTERVALS (melody note on top with a 'middle voice' completing the interval underneath).
- Beginning at bar 9* (and using bars 1–8 as an example), add your own 'middle voices' either as separate down stem notes ***(see bars 1–4)*** or as part of the up stem ***(see bars 5–8).*** Then play what you have written.

Instrument of Worship

Unknown

FOUR NOTE CHORDS have also been included in this arrangement:

F2 (bar 20)
G7 (bar 16)
Gm7 (bars 7, 9, 11, 13 and 17)

CHORD SYMBOLS

- Choose chord symbols from the following list to add above the treble staff in the interlude below. (Some may be used more than one time.)

C Csus$^4_2$ Cmaj7 C/E Dm7 E/G♯ Em/G

F F2 Fdim F/G G Gsus Am

Interlude in C

LEAD SHEETS & RHYTHM CHARTS

Sometimes the music that church musicians use is not written out *note by note.* For example, you have just seen a LEAD SHEET in your Level Five THEORY & TECHNIQUE Book which includes just a melody line plus chord symbols. But when pianists are playing in an ensemble (like a praise band) and accompanying congregational singing, they may follow a RHYTHM CHART (or CHORD CHART) that includes chord symbols. Since the singers are providing the melody, slanted lines on the staff just show the beat (or pulse) of the music.

The example below is in $\frac{4}{4}$ time and matches the lead sheet for *O COME, LET US ADORE HIM* on page 43 of your THEORY & TECHNIQUE Book.

RHYTHM CHART

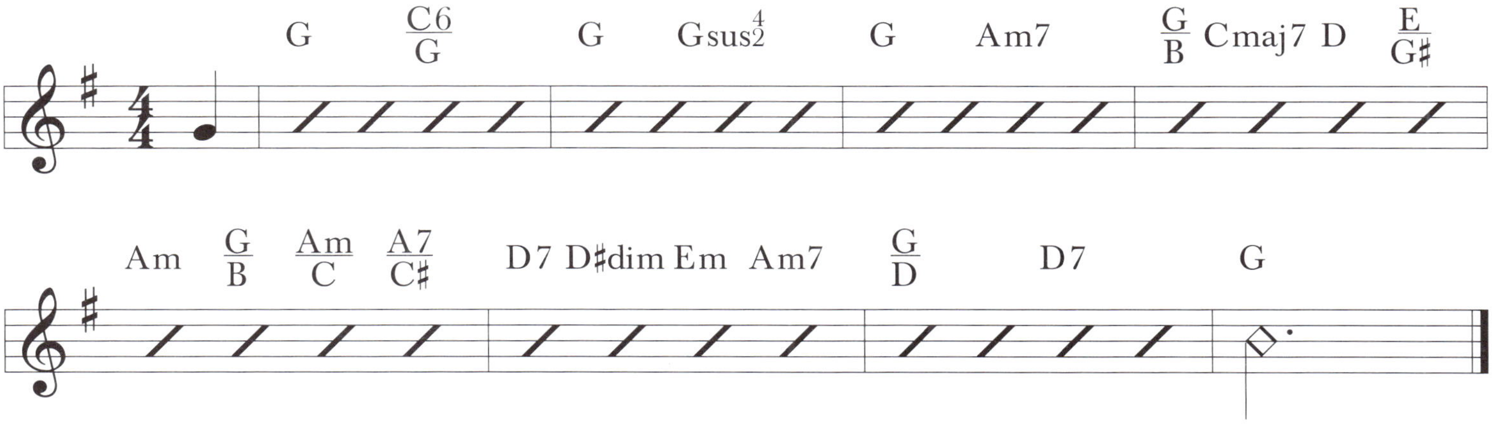

* You will often find **METRONOME MARKINGS** above the first measure in praise band 'charts'. This gives the musicians an idea of the best approximate tempo for the song. (It is a good idea to play with a metronome and/or an instrumental group when possible to help you learn to play at a steady, even tempo.)

(More about METRONOME MARKINGS on page 44 of your Level Five THEORY & TECHNIQUE Book.)

As you continue to make music throughout your life, remember how important the *IMAGINATION* factor is! Here is an opportunity to 'use' your imagination by making your own musical choices in another *brand new* arrangement of an *'old friend'!*

Jesus Loves Me

TEMPO

COMPOSER

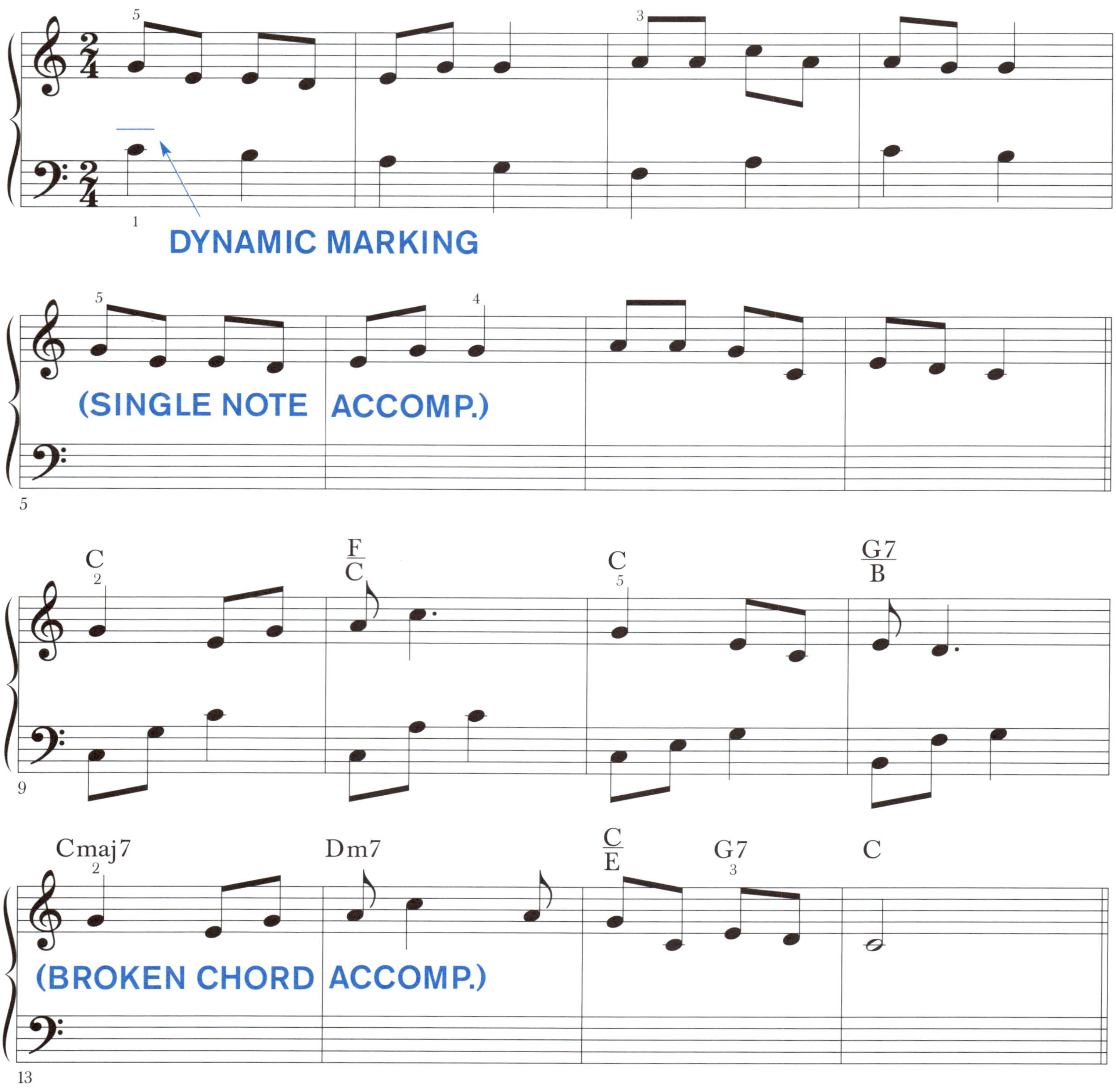

Caug C6 C7 F F/C C
17
(BLOCK CHORDS)
Cmaj7 C7 F F♯dim C/G G C
21
(DECORATED MELODY)
F/C C
25
(BROKEN CHORD ACCOMP.)
G7/B C7 F F♯dim
28
C/G E/G♯ Am D7 C/G G7 Csus C
31
(BLOCK CHORDS)
TEMPO

The MUSIC IN ME

Don't forget...

- KEY SIGNATURE
- TIME SIGNATURE
- DYNAMICS
- TEMPO
- CHORD SYMBOLS

Remember to use a pencil!

____________________'s Song

(your name)

Pedal harmonically

ff

$\frac{6}{8}$

B♭ Major?

G♭ Major?

B/F♯

Faug.

Csus$^{4}_{2}$

$\frac{6}{8}$

Dm7

B Major?

pp

¢

Gsus

$\frac{9}{8}$

AB

Cm

THY WORD

1) "Every good and perfect ________ is from above, coming down from the Father of heavenly lights...." *(James 1:17)*

2) "Shout for joy to the Lord all the ________ . Worship the Lord with ________; come before Him with ________ songs." *(Psalm 100:1–2)*

3) "The virgin will be with child and will give birth to a Son, and they will call Him Immanuel which means ______ ______ ______ ." *(Matthew 1:23)*

4) *I Corinthians 14:4* says: "But everything should be done in a fitting and ______________ way."

5) "Be joyful always; pray continually; give ________ in all circumstances, for this is God's will for you in Christ Jesus." *(I Thessalonians 5:16)*

6) "Christ loved _____ and gave Himself for _____ ." *(Ephesians 5:2)*

7) "A new __________ I give you: love one another. As I have loved you, so you must love one another." *(John 13:34)*

8) *I Chronicles 16:29 says:* "Worship the Lord in the splendor of His _________ ."

9) "Whoever loves ______________ loves knowledge...." *(Proverbs 12:1)*

10) "The fear of the Lord is the ________________ of knowledge, but fools despise __________ and discipline." *(Proverbs 1:7)*

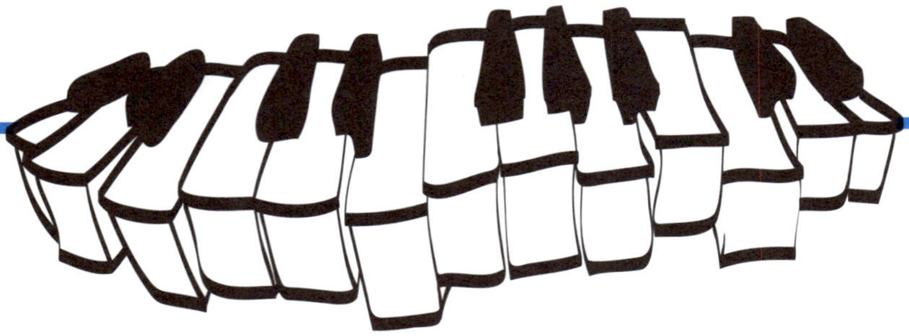

Certificate

MUSIC IN ME

"Whatever you do, work at it with all your heart...." *(Colossians 3:23)*

Congratulations!

____

has completed **MUSIC IN ME CREATIVITY BOOK (Level Five).**

TEACHER ______________________________ DATE __________